THE WELFARE STATE:

who is my brother's keeper?

The Insight Series
Studies in Contemporary Issues
from Glencoe Press

PROBLEMS OF AMERICAN FOREIGN POLICY
Martin B. Hickman

THE OPPENHEIMER AFFAIR:
a political play in three acts
Joseph Boskin and Fred Krinsky

THE POLITICS OF RELIGION IN AMERICA
Fred Krinsky

THE WELFARE STATE:
who is my brother's keeper?
Fred Krinsky and Joseph Boskin

OPPOSITION POLITICS:
the anti—new deal tradition
Joseph Boskin

IS AMERICAN DEMOCRACY EXPORTABLE?
Edward G. McGrath

PROTEST FROM THE RIGHT
Robert A. Rosenstone

DEMOCRACY AND COMPLEXITY:
who governs the governors?
Fred Krinsky

FERMENT IN LABOR
Jerome Wolf

AMERICAN ANTI-WAR MOVEMENTS
Joseph Conlin

THE POLITICS AND ANTI-POLITICS OF THE YOUNG
Michael Brown

URBAN RACIAL VIOLENCE IN THE TWENTIETH CENTURY
Joseph Boskin

POSTWAR AMERICA:
the search for identity
Donald G. Baker and Charles H. Sheldon

BLACK POWER:
the radical response to white America
Thomas Wagstaff

THE MEXICAN-AMERICANS:
an awakening minority
Manuel P. Servín

THE SUPREME COURT:
politicians in robes
Charles H. Sheldon

Series Editors: Fred Krinsky and Joseph Boskin

THE WELFARE STATE:
who is my brother's keeper?

Fred Krinsky and Joseph Boskin

Professor
Department of Political Science
University of Southern California

Associate Professor
Department of History
University of Southern California

GLENCOE PRESS
A Division of The Macmillan Company
Beverly Hills, California

CONTENTS

CONTENTS

Preface

For practical purposes, a great debate that occupied Americans during the 1930's and 1940's is now pointless: regardless of whether or not we *should* be, we clearly *are* a welfare state, if a welfare state is one that accepts responsibility for the basic economic security and physical health of all its citizens. Particularly since the Republican Administration of President Eisenhower accepted, even in theory, most of the social welfare programs bequeathed to it by twenty years of Democratic administrations, the argument over the welfare concept has been relegated to occasional academic halls and political fringe groups.

This book, though it presents the major arguments for and against the philosophy of the welfare state, concentrates primarily on presenting different views of its causes and consequences and cogent discussions of the directions its future might take. The opening chapter briefly assesses the current extent of welfare programs and sketches in the outlines of the debate over their value. Chapter Two uses the accounts of eminent scholars to describe the history of welfare programs in the United States and the climactic events of the Great Depression which brought about the creation of the American welfare state. The third chapter depicts the subsequent consensus through which most Americans have come to accept the welfare state in principle as in the breach. And finally there is a chapter which suggests new problems coming to the fore in the 1960's as the welfare concept is broadened in application through poverty programs.

Other Insight Series books deal with questions related to the growth of public welfare: labor organization, the expansion of centralized power, the nature of opposition in American politics, the polarization of radical politics on the left and right. But at the center of all these problems is the fact of welfare, and the philosophy of equal economic opportunity upon which it, and much else that is essential to American ideals, depends.

F. K.
J. B.

Los Angeles, California
November, 1967

(NOTE.—Throughout this book, the author–editors' footnotes are marked by symbols— *, †—and the original quoted notes by numerals.)

THE WELFARE STATE:

who is my brother's keeper?

Chapter One

The Nature of
The Welfare State

Of all challenges to the American interpretation of democratic ideology perhaps none is more serious than that of economic insecurity. There was a time when it appeared that despite recurring recessions the tremendous expansion of productive capacity in the United States could provide the material base for political freedom and stability without governmental intervention in the economy. Then came the Great Depression of the 1930's. The Depression indicated to Americans how serious were the potential threats to a democratic society based on an economy of abundance.

Even after thirty-five years of government regulation and planning in the economic sphere, modification of the cycle of boom and depression that characterizes capitalist economies has occurred only with the help of massive defense spending and post-war prosperity. The unrest of the impoverished minorities in the 1960's indicates further that all is not well in the welfare state.

Assuming agreement that depressions and pockets of poverty are neither desirable nor inevitable occurrences, and that men have the right and ability to control their economic destinies, the choice of the means by which full employment and prosperity can be maintained presents perplexing problems. This matter of choosing methods involves political and philosophical, as well as economic, considerations. At one level it is a question of protecting individual freedom while providing individual economic opportunity and security. But what kind and degree of security, and whose freedom?

Which groups in our society shall be the beneficiaries of public policy? On perhaps the deepest level it is a question of where the United States wants to go. What kind of a society do we really desire? We apparently have the technical capacity to make the good life possible for all citizens, but what is *the good life?*

The idea of equality in opportunities for self-fulfillment has been one of the basic themes underlying democratic social philosophy. In this context the ideal is not absolute equality but rather equal opportunity to move up the social, political, and economic ladders as much as individual ability and desire may dictate, unshackled by considerations of class, color, or initial economic condition. This implies not only that all citizens be equal before the law, but, at least to some, that the laws prevent the powerful from tyrannizing the weak.

The welfare state is our society's way of balancing the needs of strong and weak individuals, business enterprise, and the total economy. It is based on the assumption that the success of business need not be at the expense of, nor deny the legitimacy of, the needs and happiness of individuals; that governmental efforts are as legitimately applied to serving the needs of individuals in developing the good life as to promoting and protecting the interests of corporate economic enterprise. It is inevitable that in any culture some people will not have the foresight, desire, or ability to provide for themselves and will eventually become burdens on their families or society. Each society, for the common good, is compelled to provide for them somehow, and in our system it is government that acts for society in this respect.

Despite the bitter claims of some of the opponents of the particular form of adjustment that evolved during the Depression, the terms *welfare state* and *socialism* are not interchangeable. A socialist society may certainly employ welfare measures, but welfare states are not necessarily socialistic. A welfare economy does not by definition employ the socialist device of public ownership of the means of production and distribution. This is demonstrated by our own system, which can be described as a *mixed economy.* The American economy contains elements which can be classified at various points along a continuum from pure socialism to pure laissez-faire capitalism. Many enterprises popularly labeled *private* or *free* actually involve a greater degree of government control than some of the supposedly socialized sectors. For instance, there is more government control in public utilities (usually called free enterprise ventures) than there is in government contracts with private constructors of public housing projects (which are often cited as prime examples of creeping socialism). Thus it is increasingly unfruitful to characterize all welfare programs and government economic controls as *socialism.* As any self-avowed socialist will complain, our welfare state tends to eschew the public ownership of productive means in favor of central planning and indirect influence.

Though our graduated income tax has the effect of redistributing personal income, this is not a goal of the welfare state, but instead a means of achieving equality of opportunity and at least a minimum standard of living. This minimum living standard has come to imply not only a modicum of material security but also a psychological component, individual self-respect—which harks back to the traditional American concern for personal freedom. In many ways, modern proponents of welfarism are speaking for the same ideals that actuated the conservative resistance to welfare programs during the period of industrialism's first growth in the United States.

Before 1933, twentieth-century presidents tended toward the nineteenth-century liberal doctrine of laissez-faire economics—the idea of leaving businesses free to regulate their own affairs, which we now label *conservative* because it is an old one. Former President Herbert Hoover was voicing one of the cardinal precepts of conservatism in response to Franklin Roosevelt's famous "Four Freedoms" speech (1941), when he added a fifth freedom, economic freedom, to F.D.R.'s list. Hoover accepted the importance of freedom of expression and religion, freedom from fear and from want; but without economic freedom as well, he said, the other four freedoms were impossible. Though Hoover was not suggesting a return to complete laissez faire, he felt that citizens "must be free to engage in enterprise so long as each does not injure his fellow man." Among other important conservative economic values are the convictions that (1) liberty is more important than economic security; (2) government should function with maximum thrift and efficiency, and within its existing means; and (3) primary responsibility for material welfare lies with the individual, the community, and the several states, not with the federal government. Most advocates of federal welfare programs would have little serious argument with these beliefs. They do not necessarily lead to a rejection of the idea that the federal government should function to promote the welfare of its people.

The Great Depression, however, prompted the American people to reject conservative priorities and to elect a president who promised emergency measures to help the economically prostrate country. Because of the inability of local agencies to meet the economic crisis and the human problems attendant upon it, the federal government intensified its activity in the economic and social affairs of the nation.

New Deal policy consisted of emergency measures (described later) which were designed to get the economy moving as soon as possible. While the programs were not enthusiastically endorsed by conservatives, the situation was critical enough to win their temporary acquiescence. After the Depression had been replaced by a booming war economy, many of the temporary relief measures evolved into permanent programs—but acceptance by the staunchest conservatives was withdrawn.

Thus, while for over thirty years liberals have openly built government programs on the welfare approach, conservatives have swallowed these measures only as bitter pills. Conservative spokesmen have feared that the end result of so much welfare legislation will be a collectivist society in which individual initiative and national spirit might be suffocated. After a lengthy period of confused readjustment to the new fact of federal welfare, conservatism has emerged recently with articulate spokesmen like William F. Buckley, Russell Kirk, John Dos Passos, and Barry Goldwater. Their basic position is that welfare for the needy is best provided through private means, individual or co-operative, or by local government programs.

It is important to note that much conservative criticism is directed against measures like Social Security, unemployment insurance, and the graduated income tax, while many regulatory and supporting functions of government escape this opprobrium. Subsidies to small farmers and laws to protect small businessmen are, however, just as important to the concept of the welfare state as are medical payments to the aged and disabled and child support for unwed mothers. All aspects of government intervention in economic life—including highway construction and the support of basic contract law by the courts—may be seen as integral to the modern welfare state. The same tax structure that discriminates against giant individual incomes also grants depletion allowances to the oil producers.

The debate will continue, but the evidence is quite clear that the competitive struggle for political power has resulted in the development of a long-term public policy of active government participation in the economic and social life of each American. A deeper understanding of the workings and the ideology of our welfare state is necessary to every citizen who wishes to use his vote conscientiously.

The reading selections for this first chapter set out the basic facts about welfare in the modern United States. A significant article by Morris K. Udall, a Democratic congressman, argues that even if the federal government is a welfare state, its expenditures in this area are small compared with disbursements in other sections of the budget. A brief but more detailed breakdown of the welfare budget for 1967 is provided by the Friends Committee on National Legislation, with comments about the effects upon it of rising spending for the Vietnam conflict.

A final selection by Asher Achenstein, published in 1950, helps the reader to chart a course through the rhetoric and argumentation that the welfare state has occasioned and will continue to arouse. Even if welfarism is an accomplished fact, there will probably always be disagreement over its role in a society that thinks of itself as capitalistic and democratic.*

---

* Parts of this introduction appeared originally in *The Theory and Practice of American Democracy* by Fred Krinsky and Gerald Rigby. © 1967 by Dickenson Publishing Company, Inc., Belmont, California. Reprinted here by permission of the publisher.

Where's the Welfare State? (1962)*

Morris K. Udall

In January the Bureau of the Budget published its annual best-seller, "The Budget in Brief," an analysis of federal spending plans for the fiscal year starting July 1, 1962. In this fiscal year it was estimated this nation's Gross National Product would reach $570 billion. Federal receipts were to be $93 billion and federal expenditures $92.5 billion, or roughly 16 per cent of the total value of all goods and services produced by individuals and corporations during the year. Today it appears the $570 billion figure was overly optimistic and that the total will be about $555 billion, a new high but not enough to save us from a loss of tax revenue and a deficit rather than a surplus.

The budget pamphlet explains where these tax funds will be spent. Going through the list of budget items, one can see rather quickly that the expenditures fall into two categories: (1) those which are caused by the needs of national security, including preparation for war (which we hope will never come) and paying the costs of *past wars*, and (2) all other expenditures.

National Defense ....$52.7 billion
(57 cents of the tax dollar)
Cost of armed services, ships, planes, missiles,
atomic energy, military assistance, research activities. Military foreign aid is included here.

Space Research & Technology ....2.4 billion
(2.5 cents of the tax dollar)

Interest on Public Debt ....9.4 billion
(10 cents of the tax dollar)
Public debt jumped from $1 billion to $25 billion
level after World War I, to $270 billion level after
World War II. Our present public debt is almost
wholly caused by involvement in two great wars,
plus Korea and the "Cold War."

---

* From the *New Republic* (October 1, 1962), 13–14. Reprinted by permission of the *New Republic*, © 1962, Harrison–Blaine of New Jersey, Inc.

International Affairs & Finance ....3.0 billion
(3¼ cents of the tax dollar)
All the activities directed toward maintenance of
peace and strengthening free world alliances. Economic aid of $2.5 billion is included here—the only
real controversial item in the "national security"
field.

Veterans' Services & Benefits ....5.3 billion
(6 cents of the tax dollar)
VA hospitals, rehabilitation, compensation and
pensions to 4.5 million disabled veterans, widows,
orphans and other beneficiaries.

TOTAL FOR DEFENSE, DIPLOMACY AND PAST WARS ....$72.8 billion
(79 cents of the tax dollar)

Now no one would suggest that government exists only to prepare
for and fight wars. In fact, not even the outspoken critics of the
"welfare state" object to most non-defense items.

General Government ....$2.0 billion
(2 cents of the tax dollar)
Congress, courts, buildings, FBI, etc.

Natural Resources ....2.3 billion
(2.5 cents of the tax dollar)
Reclamation, flood control, national parks, mineral
resources, Indian Affairs.

Commerce & Housing ....3.4 billion
(3.5 cents of the tax dollar)
Post Office, Weather Bureau, aviation, Census,
and FHA and VA housing loans—loans which have
enabled 60 per cent of our people to own their own
homes. This category also includes the funds for
urban renewal and public housing—subjects of
some controversy—but 90 per cent of these expenditures are non-controversial.

Agriculture & National Resources ....5.8 billion
(6¼ cents of the tax dollar)
Price supports, Soil Conservation, Agricultural
Extension, Forest Service, REA, etc.

Labor, Health, Education and Welfare ....6.6 billion
(7 cents of the tax dollar)
Here it is! This is the segment of the budget which produces nearly all the controversy over "socialism" and "welfare state" spending.

TOTAL FOR NON-DEFENSE EXPENDITURES ....$20.1 billion
(21 cents of the tax dollar)

Let me point out that if *all* expenditures included in that last 7-cent "welfare state" portion of the budget were eliminated, the person who paid $1,000 income tax last year would pay $930 next year. Should they all be eliminated? No one suggests that. Should some reductions or economies be made? Here is how that 7 cents will be spent:

7¢ per $

Aid to states for the aged, blind and disabled, and for fatherless children. ....$2.9 billion

Health services and research—the National Institutes of Health, aid for hospital construction, medical scholarships, etc. ....1.4 billion

Education—federal aid for college housing and academic buildings, college scholarships, the National Defense Education Act, federal impact aid, the National Science Foundation, libraries and museums. ....1.5 billion

Labor and manpower services—on-the-job training, unemployment compensation, policing labor unions, US Employment Service, etc. ....0.3 billion

School lunch and milk program. ....0.3 billion

Vocational rehabilitation, etc.—program returning about 110,000 disabled and handicapped persons to gainful employment. ....0.2 billion

TOTAL "WELFARE STATE" EXPENDITURES ....$6.6 billion
(7 cents of the tax dollar)

I hear it said from time to time that every year this country finds itself further involved in programs of a "socialistic" or "welfare state" nature. In fiscal 1963, I remind you, we will spend 7 per cent of our federal budget (or 1.2 per cent of our GNP) for programs that are often described in this manner. How does this compare with former years?

I had the Library of Congress dig out a copy of the fiscal 1939 budget. It was an eye-opener:

—In 1939 we spent, not 7 per cent, *but 44 per cent*, of our budget for labor and welfare programs.

—In 1939 we spent $30 per capita on these programs.

—In fiscal 1963, using the 1939 dollar to provide a fixed basis of comparison, we will spend $16 per capita for these same programs.

The brutal fact is that in the past twenty-four years "welfare state" programs have withered to little more than half their pre-war level.

In 1939 this nation had 130 million people. Today we have 186 million. That we should be spending today less, in terms of 1939 dollars, than we spent twenty-four years ago is a startling revelation. Considering the 56 per cent decline in the purchasing value of the dollar since 1939, we will spend this year, in 1939 dollars, slightly over $3 billion for labor, health, education and welfare. In 1939 with 56 million fewer people, we spent nearly $4 billion. A housewife with nine children isn't expected to keep her grocery bill to the level set by her neighbor with six children, and yet that is what we as a nation have been doing. We have actually cut back our total expenditures as our population has grown.

In 1946 our federal debt per person was $1,900. Today it is down to $1,600. In 1946 out of every thousand persons in the United States, 19 were civilian employees of the federal government. Today that number has dropped to 13, and 6 of these 13 are civilian employees of the armed forces.

A further indication that the federal government is *not* growing out of proportion to our population and economy comes to light when we compare the federal debt with state, local and private debt in the United States. I doubt whether many realize that between 1941 and 1960—the last year for which figures are available—the federal debt grew just 6 per cent while state–local debt grew 328 per cent and private debt 278 per cent. Even more startling is the fact that, whereas private debt in this country was well below the federal debt in 1946, it now is more than double the federal debt.

One of the goals of traditional socialism is economic equality—"from each according to ability; to each according to need." Thus, if we are approaching socialism we should see a general leveling of society. What's happening to personal income in this country? What part does our system play in equalizing income and impeding the accumulation of wealth? Here are some pertinent facts:

—The United States, with 6 per cent of the world's population and 7 per cent of its land area has 35 per cent of all its wealth—more automobiles, telephones and other luxuries than all the other countries of the world combined.

—Personal income totals over $400 billion, with a median of $5,700 per family. But the top 5 per cent of U. S. families receive 20 per cent of all income, and the bottom 20 per cent of families receive 5 per cent of all income.

—The top 9 per cent of our population owns 46 per cent of the nation's private assets.

—Federal, state and local governments own only 12 per cent of the reproducible, tangible assets and 17 per cent of the land in the United States. All the remainder is privately owned.

A traditional goal of socialism is public ownership of mines, factories, railroads, airlines and communications. All of these key industries are privately owned in our country, in contrast to many other free nations.

"It is evident," Walter Lippmann wrote some time ago, "that creeping socialism has not crept very far."

The U.S. Budget, the War, and the Great Society (1966)*

Although the President has committed the United States to development of a "Great Society" at home and throughout Asia, he has given priority to financing the war in Vietnam. In his 1967 budget message, the President emphasized that social development was being held below "what might have been proposed in less troubled times" because "even a prosperous nation cannot meet all its goals all at once."

---

* From the Friends Committee on National Legislation, *FCNL Washington Newsletter*, No. 277 (December, 1966). Reprinted by permission.

In keeping with these priorities, Congress appropriated $84 billion, or $428 per capita, in 1966 for war, past and present; allocated another $12.8 billion for interest on the national debt (which is largely war-created), and $5 billion for explorations in space. Only $42 billion, or $214 per capita, was set aside for all other activities of the federal government. Slightly over 40 per cent of the remaining appropriations, or $88 per capita, went to provide better health, education, welfare, and housing services to Americans. Per capita allocations for foreign aid and technical assistance dropped to about the 1963 level or $13. This is less than half the amount provided for bombs and bullets. Only $1.49 per capita was appropriated for UN activities.

But these comparisons give only a partial picture of the distortions growing out of the war. According to Sen. Joseph Clark, Pennsylvania, "20 per cent of the top brains in all of the major departments of government are spending a major portion of their time on the war. . . ." The cost of living is going up, interest rates are rising, and home construction has fallen drastically.

In addition, the inadequacy of the U.S. national and international development effort has been persuasively argued by the President himself. Over the past two years, the President has deplored the plight of poor America in such words as:

—"Thirty-two million Americans remain in poverty and millions more are unable to realize their full economic potential. . . ."

—"Over four million [U.S. homes] do not have running water or even plumbing."

—"The reborn city we desire," is far away, partly because we "need to provide over 30 per cent more housing annually than we are currently building" and partly because of "our chronic inability to provide sufficient low and moderate income housing, of adequate quality at a reasonable price."

—"More than 100 million Americans have inadequate public library services. . . . Almost 70 per cent of the public elementary schools have no libraries."

—"One-third of our nation's [hospital beds] are now in obsolete condition."

·   ·   ·   ·   ·   ·   ·   ·   ·

Money Voted by Congress in 1966 for Health, Education, Welfare, and Housing [12.07% of the total, compared with 9.12% in 1964 and 12.75% in 1965].

Grants to states for dependent children, the aged, blind, and disabled................................	$ 4,081,460,000
Administrative expenses and research for welfare programs..	24,337,000
Control of juvenile delinquency.........................	8,207,000
"War on Poverty," including training, community action programs and Teacher Corps.................	1,629,500,000
Public Health Service, including grants to the states.......	2,468,326,000
Payments to trust funds for health insurance for aged (Medicare)................................	958,747,000
Indian Health, Education and Welfare...................	207,557,700
Elementary and Secondary Education Activities...........	1,526,410,000
Higher Education Activities, largely construction..........	1,147,944,000
Defense Education Act, largely aid to college students and teaching equipment............................	446,357,000
Assistance to public schools in areas where military activities are concentrated....................	480,137,000
Other education, largely vocational education.............	592,063,500
Vocational rehabilitation, including grants to the states.....	288,729,000
National Science Foundation............................	479,999,000
Museum, art and recreational commissions and D.C. institutions....................................	78,830,000
Grants to states for maternal and child welfare............	228,900,000
Children's Bureau—salaries and expenses.................	5,331,000
School Lunch Program..................................	168,605,000
Special Milk Program...................................	51,000,000
Armed Forces Dairy Program...........................	41,300,000
Agricultural donations for domestic relief and food stamp plan......................................	230,100,000
Food and Drug Administration..........................	63,130,000
Air and water pollution control.........................	268,624,000
Miscellaneous activities, including Office of Secretary, HEW.....................................	16,713,000
Housing, urban renewal and community development......	1,472,804,000
National Capital Planning Commission and Housing Authority...................................	1,072,000
Relief of natural disasters..............................	96,750,000
Estimated permanent appropriations, including $45 million for school lunch program..................	334,711,000
	$17,397,644,200

The Welfare State Debate (1950)*

Asher Achenstein

Use of the Term [*Welfare*] by Opponents of the Welfare State

The welfare state is subject to a wide variety of interpretations. If one cannot find a definition which will differentiate it from other terms, it is in part due to the fact that it is a late arrival on the political horizon. But then perhaps one should not look for definitions when the stock in trade is political oratory. In the absence of any formal definition, one must turn to the speeches and writings of those who employ the term to establish whether or not there is a common and distinct core of meaning.

Among the opponents of the welfare state, the term is used as synonymous with *statism, collectivism,* and *state socialism.* Not infrequently the same speech or article may use all three and in addition such other terms as *totalitarian state, handout state,* and *insurance state.* Common to all these terms is the idea of a centralized government undertaking more and more functions and on which citizens must come to depend increasingly for their well-being. This is in contrast to a government which assumes a minimum of functions and counts on the efforts and abilities of the individual to provide for his well-being.

.   .   .   .

Use of the Term by Supporters of the Welfare State

The proponents of the New and Fair Deals usually point out, as did President Truman in his Labor Day speech (September 5, 1949), that their opponents have adopted the age-old device of the "scare word" campaign to hide the weakness of their case. He went on to say that

> Scare words change with the times.
> When Franklin D. Roosevelt and the New Deal saved our country from the Great Depression, the selfish interests raised the scare words of *socialism* and *regimentation.*
> But the American people didn't scare.

.   .   .   .

* Asher Achenstein, *The Welfare State* ["Public Affairs Bulletin," No. 83 (Washington, D.C.: Library of Congress Legislative Reference Service, June, 1950)], pp. 3–7, 19–22, 27–28, 31–35, 37–40.

The protagonists of the welfare state claim that their opponents do not hesitate to favor governmental aid to business but shy away from assistance to the underprivileged. They point to Reconstruction Finance Corporation and Export–Import Bank Loans to business; protective tariffs which benefit particular industries, low postal rates especially on second-class mail, air-mail subsidies, and the like. They insist that the central issue in the welfare state controversy revolves around the question of "whose welfare."

The advocates of the welfare state maintain that the government must provide security for the individual against risks over which he has no control. Only by doing so can a democracy avoid the totalitarian state.

.   .   .   .

Following in the wake of our severe economic breakdown after 1929, people everywhere turned to the federal government for relief and greater security. Because every section suffered from the Depression there was almost universal demand and support for the use of the powers of the federal government to alleviate the situation. Beginning in 1933 the federal government vastly increased its responsibilities in the fields of public aid, working conditions, conservation, farming, and housing. It is now seeking to enter more energetically in the fields of education and health.

The trend toward extension of governmental powers has not only characterized the United States but also every industrialized democratic country. It started earlier in England, where the industrial revolution got under way sooner. As A. V. Dicey has shown in his classic book, *Law and Public Opinion in England*, social legislation played an increasing role in that country long before a socialist government came into power. All was regarded as not perfect in the workings of the competitive free enterprise system and it was accepted as the duty of government to correct its weaknesses. Restrictions were placed upon the individual in economic matters in the interest of achieving greater equality of opportunity for the less fortunate.

Impact of Science and Technology Upon Changing Functions of the State

Why did the increasing powers of the state take place? The answer given by those who see the necessity for further extension of government powers is science and technology. Industrialism not only made possible the rapid growth of population but also brought about the concentration of population in urban centers. A city population became dependent for its livelihood and conditions of work upon factories and upon distant markets for the sale of its products. These firms increased in size with the advantages of large-scale production and the requirements of the machine technology. Corporate enterprises began to dominate increasing areas of economic activity, culminating in the concentration of control by a few firms of the production and prices of their industries. Industrial policies were adopted restricting competition.

In congregating people into cities the machine was directly and indirectly responsible for overcrowding and for conditions creating the problems of slums. In the absence of adequate municipal regulation of land utilization, housing was constructed which in a generation became known as blighted areas. Factories could belch forth their smoke upon the surrounding dwellings without let or hindrance. Tenements were erected without adequate light and air or decent sanitary facilities. As a result of unregulated site utilization and the lack of zoning and city planning, we have a heritage of miles of slum areas today which many believe cannot be reconstructed without the cooperation of the federal government.

Science and technology also require a greater amount of schooling than was necessary in a pre-industrial civilization. The multiplicity of highly diverse occupations called forth by modern machines and appliances requires a broader schooling than the traditional "three R's." Although America has been outstanding in the world for providing free schooling for more than a century, the fact remains that areas of the country which have not benefited from the higher incomes obtained in highly industrialized areas, or from sections rich in raw materials or minerals essential to manufacturing, can afford to spend relatively little for public education. With some children receiving no elementary education at all and a larger number a very substandard education, many persons who are concerned about developing an intelligent citizenry are seeking for ways of equalizing educational opportunities. They are convinced that this objective cannot be achieved without federal aid to public education.

Another impact of science and technology has been the decline in the death rate. The improvement of the standard of living which the rapid strides in productivity made possible and the advance in medical knowledge and hygiene have greatly prolonged the average length of life. Industry, however, tends to give preference in employment to younger people. This has augmented the problem of affording security to the old aged and their dependents.

Despite the average yearly rise in productivity and in per capita income, the earnings of large masses of people are insufficient to enable them to obtain good housing, provide for the schooling of their children, lay aside a sufficient amount each year to take care of old age, meet the needs of medical care, or to provide for the hazards of unemployment.

An industrial civilization is a highly interdependent one. Markets extend beyond national boundaries. A decline in industrial activity in one country causes a quick reaction in another country thousands of miles away. Dislocations in one segment of the national economy cause reverberations in other segments. As a consequence, industrialized nations have been subject to periodic swings of prosperity and depression. In the United States, for example, there were twenty cycles of expansion and contraction between 1857 and 1937. The duration and intensity of the swings have varied from cycle to cycle. The havoc caused by the Great Depression of the 1930's in this and other countries has accentuated the cry for economic security. And many believe that the fate of democracy itself depends upon our ability to control the business cycle. It is this problem more than any that has led to wide discussion of national planning.

.   .   .   .

The Issues of Freedom versus Security

The issues which divide men and women on the welfare state originate in the fact that its philosophy and program require the further expansion of the powers of government, especially the federal government. Its supporters regard the enactment of federal legislation to increase individual security as a necessary condition for the exercise of freedom. Its opponents look upon the multiplication of centralized controls as producing a decline of liberty and the weakening of the moral fiber of the nation. One group sees in such legislation a widening of individual opportunity; the other group regards it as weakening individual responsibility.

The problem of security versus freedom has its economic as well as political aspects. The upholders of the welfare state look upon the extension of governmental powers as a necessary condition for the preservation of the free enterprise system; its opponents maintain that strengthening of these tendencies spells the ultimate doom of free enterprise.

Supporters of the welfare state, as well as those who are against it, avow that they wish to maintain the free enterprise system. Their economic differences arise from different evaluations of the effect of the extension of governmental powers upon the functioning of the economic system. Those who are against greater governmental controls argue that such expansion destroys incentives for investment, fosters an inflexible price system, makes necessary increased taxation and deficit financing, and creates a situation that inhibits technological progress. In short, according to its opponents, the welfare state not only strengthens the tendencies for restricting freedom of individuals through an expanding government bureaucracy, but it also raises doubts as to the ability of the economy to maintain the rate of economic progress which we have known in the past and which has produced an ever increasing standard of living for the American people. These are some of the problems that must be weighed by those who use the slogans of the welfare state and kindred labels.

The Individual and the State as Viewed by Proponents of the Welfare State

Underlying the views of the proponents of the welfare state are concepts of the individual and the state which differ from those held by many of its opponents. The doctrine of individualism as self-help is replaced by the view that unless social conditions are devised in which free individuals can thrive, talk about individualism is only an apology for the status quo.

.   .   .   .

In the place of *negative freedom* in the sense of non-interference by the state, modern social philosophers stress *positive freedom* by which is meant that government must provide the opportunities for every individual to realize the potentialities of which he is possessed. The emphasis upon the idea that freedom is meaningless without the state providing the conditions necessary for self-realization began to appear in the 1870's in the writings of English political philosophers like T. H. Green and F. H. Bradley. Instead of pitting the individual against the state these thinkers argued that individuality can only be achieved through society; self-realization is socially conditioned.

Liberty has long been associated with equality and in more recent times with security. In the words of the philosopher Spinoza: "It is certain that if equality of citizens be once laid aside, liberty perishes." In democratic countries great strides were made in the nineteenth century in achieving political equality. In the twentieth century stress has been laid upon economic equality.

The principle of equality does not signify that men are equal in personal qualities but rather that government must seek to provide more or less environmental equality with respect to conditions of health, education and economic security.

.   .   .   .

Inequalities produce jealousy and discord. Those who are economically at a disadvantage are pitted against the more favored and privileged. Class differences and clashes of economic interest involve struggles for power with each group attempting to further its ends through control of the state.

In recent years particular emphasis has been given to the question of economic security. Although science and technology give promise of liberating man from the bondage of insecurity, his mind seems to be preoccupied more than ever with insecurity. Whatever may be the causes of this concern, the fact remains that more and more persons have turned to the state as the agency for the removal of inequalities and the provider of basic securities. In many democratic countries, like the United States, Great Britain, the British self-governing dominions, and in the Scandinavian countries, political parties have sensed this situation, accepted it, and made it the vehicle of their assumption of power. There has been a vast increase in legislation intending to provide greater security by various devices, including the socialization of certain industries and services, the provision of goods and services based on needs, and the extension of taxation based on ability to pay to finance these new and increasing activities.

According to the political scientist Charles E. Merriam, the function of the state consists in providing security, order, justice, welfare, and freedom. Recognizing that the term *welfare* is very vague, he asks the question: "What is 'welfare' and how shall we know it when we see it?" His reply to this question is likely to be fully endorsed by the exponents of the welfare state:

> The answer is not so difficult if we bear in mind that the state is not the only human association dealing with and promoting human welfare; there is also the family, the church, and a multitude of other associations concerned with welfare in one form or another. They may, and often do, and should indeed, overlap the activities of the political society at times. But the state's interpretation of welfare is set in the constellation of security, order, justice, and freedom in a manner differing from the other societies of which men are a part, just as the state itself is set in a group of other societies as an institution.
>
> What the state does chiefly is (1) to make sure that other institutions are functioning in their own fields of welfare; (2) to pro-

mote welfare where other institutions cannot function; (3) to press forward the welfare of the whole group, as distinguished from special groups, and the welfare of all persons in the society as distinguished from the welfare of persons as members of special groupings; and (4) to aid neglected persons and groups of various kinds.

This will not provide a precise demarcation of what is or what is not welfare in particular instances, but it will give a general standard or guide. The understandings and the institutions which implement welfare in the several societies are of paramount importance in practical determination of specific courses of action. But of greater meaning is the spirit, the general direction, of welfare in a time and place.

The welfare function of the state, old and new, does not consist solely or even principally in the aggregation of a wide variety of special "services" but rather in (1) increasing the productive power of the state, the total national income; (2) establishing minimum standards of living for all, based upon productive possibilities; (3) utilizing the advances made by modern technology, physical and social, in education, medicine, personality adjustment, a broad range of possibilities in the field of invention; and (4) making possible the fullest and highest development of human personality in the framework of social relations. [1]

The Individual and the State as Viewed by Opponents of the Welfare State

Opponents of the welfare state may accept the definition of freedom as the realization of the highest potentialities of the individual but they balk at the idea that we must greatly extend the powers of government to make this possible. They are much more fearful of the power of the state and the dangers to our freedom which such powers would entail. They are fond of quoting the statement of Lord Acton that "power corrupts and absolute power corrupts absolutely." Moreover they stress the virtues of initiative, independence, choice, and responsibility. They look upon government guaranteeing economic securities to all as ushering in the Santa Claus state. They see the impulse toward liberty losing its force and being replaced by the passion for security. This is illustrated in the following quotation from a speech by Dr. Vannevar Bush, president of the Carnegie Institution:

---

[1] Charles E. Merriam, *Systematic Politics* (Chicago: University of Chicago Press, 1945), p. 54.

But if we are deluded into believing that security of the individual against all hazards and all ills can be obtained by fiat and by law, without limit, and without deliberate progress toward an end, we will sacrifice the foundation which makes humanitarianism possible, and start the weary climb over again, only after a long dark interval.

The dangers of rushing headlong into a full welfare state are very practical and very immediate. Yet there is a more subtle danger than this in the present cry for personal security. A passion for personal security is an opiate which tends to destroy the virile characteristics which have made us great. . . .

If we want a system in which, by every artifice we can command, we protect the individual citizen against all the ills of nature and of grasping man, we can have it.

We can legislate, and set up new bureaus, systemize life to the utmost, plan and regulate, until we are insured against the hazards of existence and the injustice of our fellows in every way that we can devise. But when we have succeeded in doing so we shall have produced a dead level of existence far below our possibilities—we shall have stopped progress. [2]

.   .   .   .

Those who are critical of the extension of government powers argue that the goal of providing economic equality and security means giving increased authority to a governing minority. Men in control of vast government bureaucracies tend to "forget what actual human beings are like, and try to fit men into systems rather than systems to men." Economic freedom is best safeguarded by giving free play to the competitive market. We are much more likely to preserve our liberties through the impersonal character of a competitive price system than through central direction of a government bureau. The market registers the individual choice of millions of individuals while a method of social organization where the state regulates and controls industry and trade registers the choice of a small group in the higher echelons of a government department. Those who fear the welfare state look upon the free market as a necessary safeguard of freedom and democracy and therefore seek to keep governmental interference to a minimum. Because they pin their faith upon the free market to preserve our liberties they have a different concept of the state from those who believe that such faith can only have meaning under agrarian

---

[2] *New York Times* (November 3, 1949), 19.

pioneer conditions. As one of the champions of the uncontrolled free market defines the state, it is

> ...essentially an apparatus of compulsion and coercion. The characteristic feature of its activities is to compel people through the application or the threat of force to behave otherwise than they would like to behave....
>
> The people handling the state machinery may take over other functions, duties, and activities. The government may own and operate schools, railroads, hospitals, and orphan asylums. Such activities are only incidental to the conception of the state. Whatever other functions it may assume, the state is always characterized by the compulsion and coercion exercised. [3]

It would be unjust to many, if not most, persons who consider themselves opponents of the welfare state not to mention that they do not subscribe to the extreme view of Mises that the essence of the state is coercion. They may readily endorse the view that the function of the state is to promote the general welfare and yet differ from the proponents of the Fair Deal in believing that it is not necessary to extend the powers of the federal government. While not questioning that it is the duty of government to take steps to promote the general welfare, they assert that this only poses problems but does not solve them. They may sympathize with the desire to provide against all the contingencies of life by abolishing want and unemployment and developing programs for health, old age, etc., but they believe that they are mindful of certain realities which are overlooked by those who seek to multiply governmental expenditures. They believe that the proponents of the welfare state are much too optimistic about our technological accomplishments, great as they are, to provide a standard of living which will assure to every family adequate food, clothing, housing, education, health, and a steady job. The power of the state to raise the standard of living is limited by what people produce. How much government can take from national income to carry out policies of redistribution of income without destroying economic incentives is a problem which they believe that the proponents of the welfare state are inclined to ignore. The latter likewise oversimplify the degree of compulsion which the individual is likely to be subject to because of the extension of the powers of the state. Excluding the more extreme opponents of the welfare state, the more moderate opposition is likely

---

[3] Ludwig von Mises, *Omnipotent Government* (New Haven: Yale University Press, 1944), pp. 46–47.

to agree with the statement that current debate centers around the question of how far must we go in expansion of governmental controls. In this country at least, it is mainly a question of degree of pace in government intervention rather than a real difference in kind. This is in contrast to debates about the welfare state in England where the question of nationalization of industry is a basic issue.

Chapter Two

The Depression,
The New Deal, and Keynes:
The Emerging Welfare State

As indicated by the excerpt from Ralph E. Pumphrey's thorough historical account, reprinted in this chapter, the scope of federal involvement in the area of social welfare was very limited before the 1930's. In October, 1929, however, the stock market Crash shook the nation, and from that time until the beginning of World War II a decade later the country was caught in the throes of the worst depression of the twentieth century. A selection by Robert Heilbroner sketches the causes of this catastrophe.

Few persons were prepared psychologically or financially for the effects of the economic breakdown, but city dwellers were hardest hit. Many who lived in the expanding urban centers were recent arrivals. Only in 1921 had an immigration act effectively stopped a flood of European immigration that brought millions of the Old World's poor to this country, most of them seeking jobs in the largest cities. The cities' swell was augmented by more millions of rural Americans, refugees from the agricultural depression of the 1920's. These two groups of recent arrivals formed the bulk of the factory workers and small businessmen who were most vulnerable to the effects of the Great Depression; they held the least secure jobs, and had the least savings, experience, and educational background to draw upon.

As the thirties wore on, the middle and upper classes were affected more seriously as their savings began to give out and the chain reaction of economic dislocation moved along. Factories shut down, businesses failed, schools closed for lack of funds. Hundreds of thousands of transients roamed the country look-ing for work, sleeping in doorways, hunting food in garbage cans. There were hunger riots by school children and the unemployed, strikes and attacks against the authorities by farmers and workers.

The sociological effects of the Depression on the nation during its first years are treated in a graphic manner by Frederick Lewis Allen in his book, *Since Yesterday*. In the excerpt reprinted in this chapter, he details the difficulties and failures experienced by President Hoover's Administration and the country as a whole. During this period the possibility of social revolution seemed real, even to members of the upper classes, and capitalism was commonly thought to be on its last legs.

But the pessimisms which afflicted the country in the first three years were swept away by one of the most far-reaching of political programs, Roosevelt's New Deal. The dynamic aspects of the New Deal squelched talk of revolution and nurtured a new mood of enthusiasm and hope for American capitalism and de-mocracy. It was to be expected, however, that the type of capitalism that existed prior to the Crash and Depression would have to be altered to rectify flaws in the system and to meet the needs and demands of an interdependent, complex, urban–industrial society.

The program Roosevelt launched was continually challenged by dissident groups in society who called for other solutions for the faltering economy: Senator Huey Long of Louisiana, the "Kingfish," announced a program entitled "Share the Wealth"; Father Charles Coughlin called for the nationalization of the banking system and of natural resources; Dr. Francis E. Townsend, allegedly spotting two old women invade a garbage pail in a Long Beach, California, alley, devised a system that would provide a monthly pension to those over the age of sixty; the Socialist Party charged that the New Deal program thwarted the real revolution by shoring up capitalism; and the Communist Party awaited the in-evitable move of the historical process towards a momentous clash of classes.*

Under pressure to solve the many socio-economic problems and to respond to the many different groups calling for a change, President Roosevelt evolved a system of *welfare capitalism*. Maintaining the basic system of capitalism, with its accent on private property and profit-making incentive, Roosevelt instituted the means by which the federal government became more alive to the social needs of the people and able to fulfill the "welfare clause" (Article I, Section 8) of the Constitution. Professor Paul K. Conkin describes the changes wrought by Roosevelt's Administrations in our selection from his fine book, *The New Deal*.

One of the most important aspects of the New Deal—and one of the least understood—is the affect of Keynesian economics. The idea of deficit spending was not an intrinsic aspect of the New Deal program. Roosevelt himself did not accept the idea of deficit spending as a permanent part of government operations

---

* For a more thorough discussion of the pattern of opposition to the New Deal and its descendant programs, see the Insight Series book by Joseph Boskin, *Opposition Politics: The Anti–New Deal Tradition*.

until after the recession of 1937–1938. Prior to the recession, Roosevelt felt that if large monies were infused into the economy on many levels, prosperity and employment would return and a balanced budget would then be achieved. The balanced budget was seldom to be accomplished, however, during the New Deal or during subsequent administrations. Debt had become an integral part of the individual, business, and governmental way of life, although it should be noted that the large debt of the federal government is due principally to defense and war spending. Professor Stephen K. Bailey, in a section of his book, *Congress Makes a Law,* succinctly analyzes the contribution of John Maynard Keynes' ideas to the economic arrangement of society.

These two phenomena, then, the Great Depression and the New Deal Program that came in response to the problems of the Depression, were the prime factors in expanding the role of the federal government in the area of social welfare. Yet it is also certain that even if the Depression had not occurred, many of today's welfare measures would have been made a part of the American system. For in the final analysis, it was not an economic tragedy that brought the national government into the area of welfare but the factors of industrialism and urbanism. In short, the needs of a modern, complex society were the underlying causes of the changes.

Social Welfare in the United States*

Ralph E. Pumphrey

Organized help for persons recognized as unable to care for themselves or meet their social obligations is found almost universally. The family or the clan is usually expected to assume primary responsibility for its own members. When help from these intimate groups is insufficient, religious organizations, voluntary associations, and agencies of government step in with social welfare provisions. Some of these provisions require payment by financially able beneficiaries, and in some cases they are organized on a commercial, profit-making basis. Such commercial activities are not generally considered to be social welfare, although their availability and effectiveness influence the provision of other social welfare services. Other activities of government and industry also influence social welfare without being considered part of it.

---

* Reprinted by permission from *The Encyclopedia of Social Work* (15th issue of the *Social Work Yearbook*), pp. 19–22, 28–29, 31–35.

The broad institutional patterns of social welfare in the United States were laid down in England before or during the period of American colonization. Two enactments of the Parliament of 1603 are usually thought to symbolize these patterns. They were the famous Elizabethan Poor Law and the Law of Charitable Uses.

The Poor Law was a codified restatement of principles evolved in the legislation of previous centuries, particularly the previous seventy-five years. It authorized governmental provision for the poor so that nobody would starve through neglect, but family responsibility was not abrogated nor idleness encouraged. Private philanthropy was not mentioned in the Poor Law, but the need for governmental assistance was often reduced by philanthropy, established under rules laid down in the Law of Charitable Uses. This law defined the conditions under which men might set aside portions of their wealth for specific charitable purposes and specified procedures for the administration of the trusts. An important supplementary measure, the Settlement Law (1662), established a minimum period of residence before a person would become legally settled in a parish (the smallest unit of government). Until this minimum period had elapsed, a needy person could be refused aid and could be forced to return to the parish where he did have settlement.

These laws, which the English colonists carried with them, embodied several distinct but interrelated ideas: the family should take care of its own, charitable individuals should help their neighbors, and when all else failed, the government of his home community must take care of a needy person. A not infrequent combination of these ideas occurred in Boston in the middle of the seventeenth century when affluent citizens made bequests for the erection of an almshouse which was to be maintained and operated by the town for the better care of the town's aged and infirm.

For more than three hundred years, governmental provision for the needy in America, as in England, was guided by the Poor Law and the Settlement Law. In the United States, colonial laws based on those of the mother country were enacted after independence. As new states drew on the experience of older ones, the Poor Law was transmitted, with a minimum of change, across the continent. Modifications did not change the essential nature of the law until well into the twentieth century, and even today general assistance provisions in the laws of many states retain much of the language of the law of 1603.

The Law of Charitable Uses and related measures were less immediately applicable on a wide scale in the colonies because it took time to accumulate individual wealth which might be bestowed as trusts. Sizable charitable bequests, such as those in Boston in 1658, did not become commonplace until much later. Early in the nineteenth century, when bequests were becoming larger and more numerous, judicial decisions in some of the states limited the ways in which benefactions might be made under American adaptations of the English law. Nevertheless, with industrial and commercial wealth accumulating in the nineteenth and twentieth centuries, benefactions became larger and more numerous and added renown to such family names as Franklin, Girard, Peabody, Carnegie, Sage, Rockefeller, and Ford.

Despite the infrequence of endowments, the idea of personal obligation which the Law of Charitable Uses sanctioned was widespread in the colonies. Wealthy persons, like George Washington, maintained their own systematic largesse. Religious leaders gave adherents opportunity to express their compassionate concerns, but this role of the church was somewhat eclipsed as time went on. More and more secular organizations were set up, often with the blessing of the church, to carry on activities, many of which originally had been integral parts of the church's obligation to its members.

Voluntary associations existed in the colonies. Some held close to the elemental concept of mutual aid, in which neighbors or associates join together to build houses, provide nursing care, or perform other services for one another. Other associations minimized mutual aid, emphasizing benevolence through relief of suffering among those less fortunate. The earliest of the voluntary associations which still exists, the Scots Charitable Society (Boston, 1657), appears to have combined both mutual aid and philanthropy in its objectives.

Even this kind of philanthropic approach implied an accumulation of disposable wealth found in prosperous urban communities rather than on the frontier. Hence associations were not common until the middle of the eighteenth century, and then in the cities—Boston, New York, Philadelphia. Characteristically, they were local in scope and provided specific goods or services, or served limited age, nationality, or religious groups. Descriptive names borne by many of them, such as Home for Little Wanderers, Penitent Females' Refuge, and Home for Intemperate Women, sound quaint today.

Developmental Patterns

Government, individual philanthropy, and voluntary associations are three types of auspices for social welfare activities which have been found throughout American history. Sometimes each has concentrated on a distinctive area of concern and has even fought for exclusive jurisdiction. Generally, however, they have not been mutually exclusive, and not infrequently all three types of effort are represented on single projects. These interrelations, however, cannot alone explain the history of the complex social welfare structure of today.

Three major themes may be followed in an effort to throw light on the historical development of social welfare:

1) Ideas of need which originally were quite simple and called for simple remedies have been replaced by complex ideas of what constitutes need, with corresponding specialized types of services.

2) A variety of ways of dealing with each need has been invented.

3) Without ever repudiating the idea of local responsibility, both governmental and non-governmental organizations have established wider and wider geographical bases for their operations.

Increased Complexity of Recognized Needs

In any frontier society the basic problem is that of physical survival. Individuals, families, and neighbors pit their resources against an environment which is often hostile and which requires cooperation merely to keep alive. Mutual aid, as it was found on the American frontier for three centuries, was therefore an expression both of altruism and of self-preservation. But mutual aid is a weak instrument on which to depend for regular services. It requires that people be available to give their help when needed, have the necessary skills, and see the danger or the need as sufficient to justify leaving their own pressing duties. Furthermore, there is always the problem of equitable distribution of the burden. Hence, it was natural for the settlers, at each stage of the westward movement, to include poor relief in their earliest governmental formulations.

The Poor Law had marked advantages over mutual aid. It recognized that persons might be in trouble for a variety of reasons, and that the responsible officials should relate the help given to the cause of difficulty. The aged and "impotent" (helpless) poor were to receive food, shelter, and care. Dependent children were to be indentured as apprentices to persons who would provide them with care and with instruction which would make them self-supporting as adults. Able-bodied persons who lacked work were to be made self-supporting through specially devised employment.

Useful as this classification was, since 1603 conscientious persons have found it difficult to make the fine distinctions between employability and unemployability among dependent children or ill or handicapped adults. When employable persons have needed help, there has also been the problem of what to expect of them in return for the help given. In practice, however, this sort of issue has come to the fore only in the larger units of administration. Since the Poor Law was administered at the smallest unit of government, often by part-time, unpaid officials, with a small burden of need in any one place, even as late as the Civil War few persons had occasion to recognize the problems as of any significance. When such recognition did occur, it was often outside the governmental structure and resulted either in an individual philanthropic gift or in the establishment of some voluntary association to deal with it.

In most colonial towns and villages under the Poor Law, food, shelter, and minimal medical care were provided for needy people. Occasionally supplementary help was given by local churches or relief societies. Arrangements were often made with families to care for helpless individuals, with reimbursement from tax funds. By the middle of the eighteenth century some localities "vendued" their poor, a practice which was still followed in rural areas a century later. At an auction the care of the poor, individually or in groups, was turned over to the person or persons who offered to do it at the least cost to the town. In more progressive communities almshouses might be established and children might be indentured. Nevertheless, one senses that in colonial and frontier America there was a fatalistic attitude toward misfortune, with little attempt to override it other than to provide necessities to keep the victim alive.

Beginnings of Specialized Services

Toward the end of the colonial period a few developments presaged changes which would become marked during the following century. In New Orleans, then under French rule, the Ursuline Sisters in 1729 set up an orphanage to care for survivors of a smallpox epidemic. In 1769, the Virginia legislature authorized the establishment of the first publicly supported mental hospital in the colonies, opened in 1773. Thus both children and the mentally ill were recognized as having special problems. The idea of isolating a cause of dependency and developing appropriate specialized services for its victims was most clearly stated, however, in the arguments developed by Benjamin Franklin in support of the Pennsylvania Hospital, established in 1750.

The then novel objectives of this hospital were: furnishing a central, well-equipped place where the best doctors could provide the most up-to-date care, thereby getting the patients back to their homes and work in the shortest possible time; and providing opportunities for medical research. Franklin stressed the benefits to taxpayers as well as to the poor patients themselves in having such care available. He thus introduced an attitude of hope for the "impotent poor."

The possibility of avoiding the cost of dependency by curing illness attracted wide attention. By the end of the eighteenth century there were hospitals in a number of cities. But not all people requiring medical care needed to be in hospitals. Again with Franklin's support, dispensaries for the outpatient treatment of illness began to appear. This choice between care and treatment for the patient within the institution (indoor aid) and for the patient who remains in his own home (outdoor aid) has been the subject of frequent and sometimes vitriolic debate in almost every field of social welfare since Franklin's time.

Despite these beginnings of change, most social welfare activity in the newly-independent United States at the opening of the nineteenth century remained centered in the Poor Law as modified from English experience and supplemented by sporadic voluntary activities. The help given by local officials was frequently criticized. In the seaboard cities the influx of immigrants with few if any resources far exceeded any institutional facilities available. Taking their lead from England, voluntary associations and state governments engaged in a series of investigations of the causes of pauperism and the effectiveness of the administration of both the Poor Law and private charities. The best known of the state investigations were those conducted by Josiah Quincy in Massachusetts in 1821 and by J. V. N. Yates in New York in 1823.

The reports of these investigations stressed a theme popular in England about the same time—that almshouses (indoor relief) were more efficient and less subject to administrative favoritism than relief given to persons in their own homes (outdoor relief), and therefore, should be established in every jurisdiction. The care given in the almshouses should be such as to deter people from applying unless they were in dire need. There followed a long period in which almshouse care was the standard of local assistance throughout the country. Recommendations in keeping with the original Poor Law, that appropriate facilities be provided for the sick and other special groups, and that work be provided for the able-bodied, were seldom observed. The typical almshouse or poor farm was a cheerless place where those who were unable to provide for themselves, of all ages, sexes, and conditions of physical and mental health, were thrown together indiscriminately.

As people in communities came to recognize the effects of almshouse neglect, movements for the establishment of classified facilities accelerated markedly. Schools for the deaf under voluntary auspices, but with federal and state aid, were established in Connecticut in 1817 and in Kentucky in 1824. The state-aided Perkins Institute for the Blind was established in Boston in 1829 and there, a few years later, the success of Samuel Gridley Howe in educating Laura Bridgman, who was both deaf and blind, had an important effect on the public attitude of fatalism toward physical disabilities.

Dorothea Dix was the great crusader against the evils of almshouse care. Her particular concern was for the "lunatics" and "idiots" whom she found helpless and cruelly abused almost everywhere she went in her wide travels. Through her efforts during the two decades preceding the Civil War, states throughout the country established lunatic or insane asylums in which, if cure was uncertain, at least care was more suitable than in almshouses and jails. In Miss Dix's reports on conditions in almshouses and jails in the various states, reformers found a wealth of information which both stimulated them to action and made easier their task of proving the need for specialized facilities. By the end of the nineteenth century most states had schools or institutions for some or all of the following: the blind, the deaf, the mentally ill, the mentally deficient, and epileptics.

.   .   .   .

Problems of Cultural and Racial Groups

Three great movements closely related to enhancement of the individual vitally affected social welfare—free public education, anti-slavery, and the incorporation of new cultural and racial groups into American society. John Griscom was one of many who feared ignorance not alone as a cause of poverty but as a threat to the soundness of judgment of the electorate under universal manhood suffrage. The campaign for free public education was at its height during the period 1820–1850. During that time the basic principle was accepted by most states. After the Civil War most efforts were directed to achieving universality, equality, extension to higher educational levels, and compulsion. As the elaborate institutional establishments of education and social welfare developed, the close ties between them sometimes became obscured. Still, their presence was constantly attested to by voluntary social welfare efforts to supply services not provided by government and to secure inclusion of such additional service in the regular school programs, for example, sight-saving classes and home instruction for handicapped children.

As success crowned the initial struggle for free education, abolition claimed much of the reforming zeal of America. The same people who were interested in free public education, the handicapped, prisoners, and children, were also interested in seeing the Negro slaves freed. For many, this became *the* compelling issue, and it is possible that the time and energy devoted to the antislavery campaign, if it had been diverted to other issues, might have moved many social welfare activities forward much faster than actually occurred.

The end of slavery brought new problems. The recolonization of freed slaves in Africa had been vigorously advocated by the American Colonization Society in the 1820's. However, after an initial few thousands had been sent to Liberia, the number had dropped to a trickle. The wholesale emancipation of slaves made continued re-colonization no more than an incidental activity. Efforts to incorporate the Negro into the nation's political life without educational and economic preparation led to the sort of undisciplined behavior that Griscom and others had feared from an uneducated electorate, and they stopped at the end of the Reconstruction Era. The reforming zeal of the abolitionists had secured the immediate objective, but the effort had proved too exhausting to leave energy for the necessary follow-up.

All efforts on behalf of the Negro did not cease, however. In the South meager public educational opportunities were supplemented by private schools, often under religious sponsorship and usually emphasizing self-help. Educational and economic opportunities improved gradually, but not as fast as for other parts of the population. Most Negroes were poorly prepared to take advantage of an upsurge of industrial employment which occurred in the twentieth century at the same time that mechanization of agriculture was driving them from their accustomed occupations. They became marginal members of society, with little incentive to seek advancement. From World War I on, the problems of educational, economic, political, and social equality for Negroes in American life became increasingly pressing.

In the industrial centers the influx of Negro population was reminiscent of many previous waves of immigration. Most European immigrants had few assets beyond their health and willingness to work.

Illness and inability to pay for transportation to the hinterland forced many to remain in the seacoast cities. By 1900 free land for homesteading was scarce and remote, so that greater capital was required to become established on the land; the industrial employment available in the cities required unfamiliar skills and cultural adjustments for persons of peasant background; and the number of immigrants was increasing to unprecedented levels. Consequently, increasingly large numbers of persons, isolated by barriers of language and custom, were huddled together in the cities, obtaining the poorest jobs, living in the poorest housing, suffering the greatest amount of illness, and furnishing a disproportionate number of social misfits, particularly in the second generation. The peak of this problem was reached in the decade before stringent restrictions on immigration were imposed in 1921.

Settlement Movement

One of the great contributions of the workers in the settlements was that they built on the previous experiences and cultural standards of the people among whom they lived and expended themselves. Starting with Stanton Coit's Neighborhood Guild (University Settlement) in New York in 1886, the movement attracted college and university men and women who "settled" in residences in crowded, poverty-stricken neighborhoods, and identified themselves with the lives and concerns of those about them. Their observations and activities resulted in the establishment of such tangible facilities and services as public baths and playgrounds, in pressure for the establishment of juvenile courts and other services, and in much of the intellectual support for economic and social reforms.

Informal education and encouragement of all forms of artistic and political expression were common in the settlements. Other organizations also developed adult educational programs. Such activities had started in the early days of the YMCA and the Sunday school and working girl movements. They received new impetus before and after World War I from the Americanization movement. Ultimately they came to be recognized as appropriate permanent parts of the public educational programs of communities, providing a broad range of subject matter, including vocational training and retraining, for people from all walks of life.

. . . .

Expansion of the Geographical Concept of Responsibility

Expanding awareness of social welfare needs and an increasing array of measures with which to meet them were accompanied by changes in attitude toward the auspices under which such measures should be carried out. To some extent there have been changes in the attitudes regarding the division of responsibility between governmental and voluntary organizations, but to a much greater extent the changes have related to the division of responsibility between different levels of government and corresponding divisions within the voluntary field. In particular, the idea of the locality as the unit within which services should be organized has been subjected to great pressure.

The English legislation of 1603 assumed that the central government had rule-making authority with respect to social welfare. This authority was assumed in America by the colonial and, later, the state governments. The problems dealt with by either philanthropy or the poor law were seen, however, as being of local magnitude. An early New York law stated: "Every city and town shall support and maintain their own poor." The smallest local unit of government (parish, township, city, county) bore residual responsibility after the exhaustion of the resources of family, mutual aid, and philanthropy. Indeed, on the frontier, poor law administration was not far removed from mutual aid.

When communications were slow, and many human emergencies were past before help could be obtained from a distance, there was little to encourage a broader outlook. Yet, as early as the seventeenth century, disaster forced recognition of wider responsibility in both relief and military administration. An Indian attack on the frontier hamlet of Deerfield, Massachusetts, in 1675, forced its abandonment for a number of years. The residents, who had suffered great loss, also had lost their legal settlements and hence could not get help in the town from which they had come. The colonial legislature ordered aid given to the victims of the raid by whatever town had given them refuge, with the colony reimbursing that town. In this way originated the idea of *state poor*, people for whom the state was responsible because they did not have settlement in any subdivision.

New York and other colonies and states adopted similar measures, first in emergencies and then as regular provision. This proved particularly important in the seacoast cities during the nineteenth century when many immigrants found themselves in need before they had time to establish settlement.

By its very usefulness, the concept of *state poor* emphasized the duality of requirements under the poor law. Not only must the applicant be needy, but also he must be eligible. Whenever this has been true, down to the present, the tendency has always been to see how many could be proved ineligible, rather than how many were needy. Until the middle of the nineteenth century this approach was widely supported by the practice of *warning out*. This ritual was derived from the settlement law authorization for returning needy persons to their places of settlement. Many places merely warned newcomers periodically that they should leave, and on this basis disclaimed financial responsibility, no matter how long they remained. In some states this practice persisted much longer. Iowa, for instance, dropped it only in 1959, and vestiges persist in the general assistance laws of other states.

Development of State Responsibility

During the nineteenth century the states gradually expanded their roles in social welfare. This was much less dramatic than in England, where the Poor Law Reform Act of 1834 significantly increased the influence of the central government by consolidating local administrative units and setting more rigid standards for local administration. The investigations by Quincy, Yates, and others established the principle of state inquiry into local affairs and threw the weight of state influence toward local institutional care in almshouses. But this influence rested lightly on the localities and the most substantial development of state responsibility prior to the Civil War came in institutional care for special groups, notably the insane, which were too few in number and too scattered for effective local provision.

Since each institution as well as each city or town was autonomous, there were still a marked lack of uniformity and frequently inadequate standards. Measures to secure greater uniformity and state control began to be adopted. In Massachusetts, in 1863, a Board of State Charities was created, composed of leading citizens appointed by the governor. Its primary responsibility was supervision of the care given to the state poor and other wards of the state in state institutions, in towns under the overseers of the poor, and by voluntary associations. It also collected information regarding all poor relief activities in the state. It used its administrative authority, which was limited at first, to transform several isolated almshouses into a pioneer system of specialized institutional and foster home care of children and insane persons.

Within ten years, ten states had adopted the idea of a state board of charities, each with variations dictated by its own poor law and institutional arrangements. By 1897 sixteen, and by 1914 thirty-eight states had state boards. As experience accumulated, these boards moved generally in the direction of centralized administrative authority over state institutions and programs. Contrary to English experience, however, localities were generally successful in resisting interference or transfer of power. Consequently, in spite of inspection and supervision of local almshouses, workhouses, orphanages, and outdoor relief programs by the state boards, the boards seldom obtained administrative control over local programs, and there remained wide variations in practices within states as well as between states.

.   .   .   .

Beginnings of Federal Activity

[In the 1840's, Dorothea] Dix clearly exposed the wide variation in financial capacity and motivation among the states and localities in social welfare matters. She proposed that the federal government assume a degree of responsibility for encouraging state action by giving public lands to the states to finance the erection of hospitals for the insane. Precedents for such action were grants of land previously made to help schools for the deaf in Connecticut and Kentucky.

In 1854 Congress passed a bill incorporating Miss Dix's proposals, but it was vetoed by President Franklin Pierce, who, as a "strict constructionist," viewed the powers of the federal government as limited in comparison with those of the states. In his veto, he strongly enunciated state and particularly local and philanthropic responsibility. The Pierce veto became the controlling doctrine in American social welfare for two generations. State boards, state and local institutions and programs, and most private philanthropy were shaped and increasingly constricted by the limits which it set.

Since the states had never previously assumed much direct responsibility in social welfare, they could expand their functions for half a century before serious questions of potentials and limits began to arise. However, many problems came to be regarded as no longer purely local. Here and there exclusive state and local responsibility was ended. Sometimes the states wanted or would accept federal help, as in the case of the Morrill Act (1862) establishing the system of land-grant colleges. Sometimes the Supreme Court declared vital functions which the states had undertaken in self-protection, such as the regulation of immigration, to be the responsibility of the federal government (1849, 1876), and Congress had to act.

Illustrations of increasing federal activity are: a rudimentary public health service in connection with foreign commerce and immigration; the collection of basic social data through the census and the federal Bureau of Labor (established in 1885); the first (1909) and subsequent White House Conferences; the creation of the U.S. Children's Bureau (1912); the Sheppard–Towner Act (1921, expired 1929) to provide federal aid to state programs in maternal and child health and welfare; two federal child labor laws, both declared unconstitutional; and a proposed child labor amendment to the Constitution.

.   .   .   .

Decline of State and Local Responsibility

Between the Pierce veto and the Great Depression of the 1930's the United States had taken its place as a highly industrialized world power with a strong central government. In social welfare, however, increased responsibilities assumed by state governments and tentative gestures by the federal government still left poverty-stricken persons dependent for help on programs much like those worked out in England in the days of Shakespeare and Ben Jonson.

Unemployment and destitution were so extensive in the early 1930's that local governments, even states, found themselves near bankruptcy. In spite of the political and social pressures inherent in this situation, it was hard to change established concepts of federal, state, and personal responsibilities. Several temporary measures were tried before the passage of the Social Security Act as permanent legislation in 1935 gave new perspectives to social welfare policy.

Social Security Act. The Social Security Act was a gigantic supplementation of the existing social welfare provisions. It projected the federal government into the solution of a number of urgent specialized problems with politically feasible measures which it was hoped would satisfy constitutional requirements. These problems included unployment, economic dependency in old age or childhood, unemployability due to physical disability, potential dependency due to illness or physical or social handicap in childhood, and threat to the public health and welfare through contagious disease.

In dealing with this wide range of problems, several methods were utilized. Individuals and communities received governmental services in the areas of public health, vocational rehabilitation, crippled children, and maternal and child health and welfare. Public assistance grants to individuals were provided for the dependent aged, the blind, and children. Insurance was to mitigate loss of income due to old age or unemployment.

In the all-important consideration of the relations between the state and federal governments a number of approaches were used. The states were enticed to establish or expand service and public assistance programs through the offer of grants-in-aid. They were coerced into establishing unemployment insurance programs through imposition of a federal tax which would be rebated in states which established such programs. The federal government, using its taxing power, itself established the insurance program to provide retirement income.

Grants-in-aid had been used in England for nearly a century. Since 1911 they had been used in the United States for such programs as highways, the National Guard, and, in a minor way, for vocational rehabilitation and maternal and child health. They required state appropriation of matching funds and compliance with program requirements set down by the federal government. There were no constitutional hurdles, and the states were left with full autonomy in those aspects of service and assistance not touched by grants-in-aid.

Insurance for loss of income, however, involved a dilemma. If it were actuarially feasible for states to operate such programs, how could employers in the states setting up such programs be protected against the lower costs of employers in the states without programs? If, on the other hand, it were necessary to use the nation as a whole as an actuarial base, how could the long-standing constitutional argument against direct federal welfare activity be overcome?

For unemployment compensation, state administration was favored. The threat of economic disadvantage was nullified by a previously tested device. The federal government imposed a uniform payroll tax on employers throughout the country. However, in those states which set up unemployment compensation programs, taxes paid to the state for this purpose could be credited against up to 90 per cent of the federal liability. The effect was to make it economically advantageous for states to establish such programs, and they did so quickly.

For old age retirement, federal administration was deemed necessary. To meet constitutional objections, the provisions for benefits and those for financing them through taxes were put in widely separated titles. There was precedent for each activity separately but none for the total operation. By introducing a number of extraneous matters between the two titles, a legal fiction was extablished that the two titles had nothing to do with each other, and hence the government was not providing insurance. The fiction was sustained by the Supreme Court in 1937 when it declared the act to be constitutional.

The legal tour de force involved in the drafting of the Social Security Act established the principle that the federal government, the states, and localities share responsibilities in social welfare. The pattern of approaches to social welfare, after being legally tested, could be elaborated and modified with reasonable assurance of constitutionality. But this tended to keep innovations to a minimum. Furthermore, the legal fiction regarding the non-insurance status of the retirement system has been the source of popular confusion and political bickering.

Expansion of the Federal Role

Changes in the Social Security Act since its enactment have resulted in vocational rehabilitation, public health, and unemployment compensation being separated out and each becoming the subject of extensive legislation. Retirement insurance has been extended to cover disability, benefits are provided for dependents as well as the wage earner, and nearly all wage earners have been brought into the system. Additional coverage, program requirements, federal participation, and other changes have been introduced into the public assistance and service programs. However, since all aspects of the act except retirement and disability insurance depend on state implementation, there remain considerable variations in programs between the states.

The passage of the National Mental Health Act of 1947 completed the reversal of the position represented by the Pierce veto of 1854. Pierce had feared that provision for the insane would open the way to federal help in public assistance. Now public assistance was a recognized function of the federal government. To Dorothea Dix's humanitarian emphasis on care and treatment were added considerations of national defense, economic benefit, and the greater potentials of joint federal-state programs for research and treatment.

Causes of the Depression*

Robert L. Heilbroner

Speculation

How did this tragedy come about?

An immediate, precipitating cause was, of course, the speculative fever which had engulfed the economy by 1929. The mania was not just confined to Wall Street. Throughout the nation, a get-rich-quick philosophy had destroyed normal business and banking caution. Foreign bonds of the most dubious validity were eagerly (and sometimes ruthlessly) pushed by the banks into investor's hands or, worse folly, put

---

* Pages 144–54 from Robert L. Heilbroner, *The Making of Economic Society*, © 1962. Reprinted by permission of Prentice–Hall, Inc., Englewood Cliffs, New Jersey.

into their own portfolios.[1] In addition, huge pyramided structures of investment trusts and holding companies erected a house of cards atop the operating base of enterprise. For instance the Georgia Power Company was controlled by the Seaboard Public Service Corporation, which was controlled by the National Public Service Corporation, which was controlled by the Middle West Utilities Company, which was controlled by Insull Utility Investments, Inc., which was controlled by the Corporation Securities Company of Chicago (which was controlled, in turn, by Insull Utility Investments, which presumably *it* controlled). Of these companies, only one—Georgia Power—actually produced electricity. The rest produced only profits and speculative opportunities. And the Insull empire was only one of *twelve* holding companies that owned 75 per cent of all the utility operating plants in the country.

All these manipulative activities helped to pave the way for the Depression. When the stock market finally crashed, it brought down with it an immense flimsy structure of credit. Individual investors who had borrowed to the hilt to buy securities had their stock sold out from under them to meet their indebtedness to brokers. Banks and financial institutions, loaded with dubious foreign bonds, were suddenly insolvent. Later, when the Depression really began, the funds of the utility operating companies which could have been used to provide employment were milked upstairs to rescue or to delay the collapse of the financial superstructure.

Weakness on the Farm

In the vulnerability of an economy bound up with a rickety and speculative financial superstructure we have located one reason for the Great Depression—or, more specifically, one reason why the Wall Street Crash pulled down with it so much business activity. But we have far from exhausted the explanations for the Depression itself. For the Crash, after all, might have been no worse than many previous speculative disasters. Why was it protracted into a chronic and deep-rooted ailment?

The question turns our attention away from the spectacular misfortunes of 1929 to a consideration of the state of the economy as a

---

[1] Many of these deals were unsavory to the point of malfeasance. The son of the President of Peru, for instance, was paid $450,000 by the securities affiliate of the National City Bank for his services in connection with a $50 million bond issue which the bank's affiliate then floated for Peru. The President's son's "services" consisted almost entirely of an agreement not to block the deal. Eventually, of course, the bonds went into default. (John K. Galbraith, *The Great Crash, 1929.* Boston: Houghton Mifflin Company, 1955, p. 186.)

whole in the years preceding the collapse. We have already characterized the first quarter of the twentieth century as a time of unprecedented
expansion. Could it be, however, that behind the overall figures of rising output and incomes there were concealed pockets of trouble?

Even during the 1929's, economists would have agreed that one
such worrisome sector existed. This was the farm sector. All through
the 1920's, the farmer was the "sick man" of the American economy.
Each year saw more farmers going into tenantry, until by 1929 four
out of ten farmers in the nation were no longer independent operators.
Each year the farmer seemed to fall further behind the city dweller in
terms of relative well-being. In 1910 the income per worker on the farm
had been not quite 40 per cent of the non-farm worker; by 1930, it was
just under 30 per cent.[2]

Part of this trouble on the farm, without question, stemmed from
the difficult heritage of the past. Beset now by drought, now by the
exploitation of powerful railroad and storage combines, now by his own
penchant for land speculation, the farmer was proverbially an ailing
member of the economy. In addition, the American farmers had been
traditionally careless of the earth, indifferent to the technology of agriculture. Looking at the average individual farmer, one would have said
that he was poor because he was unproductive. Between 1910 and 1920,
for instance, while non-farm output per worker rose by nearly 20 per
cent, output per farm worker actually fell. Between 1920 and 1930,
farm productivity improved somewhat but not nearly so fast as productivity off the farm. For the great majority of the nation's agricultural producers the trouble appeared to be that they could not grow
or raise enough to make a decent living.

If we had looked at farming as a whole, however, a very different
answer would have suggested itself. Suppose that farm productivity
had kept pace with that of the nation. Would farm income as a whole
have risen? The answer is disconcerting. The *demand* for farm products
was quite unlike that for manufactured products generally. In the
manufacturing sector, when productivity rose and costs accordingly
fell, the cheaper prices of manufactured goods attracted vast new
markets, as with the Ford car. Not so with farm products, however.
When food prices fell, people did not tend to increase their actual
consumption very greatly. Increases in overall farm output resulted
in much lower prices but not in large cash receipts for the farmer.

---

[2] E. A. J. Johnson and Herman E. Krooss, *The American Economy* (Englewood
Cliffs, N.J.: Prentice–Hall, Inc., 1960), p. 351.

Faced with what is called an *inelastic demand*, a demand which does not respond in proportion to price changes, a flood of output only left the farm sector *worse* off than before.

That is very much what happened during the 1920's. From 1915 to 1920, the farmer prospered because World War I greatly increased the demand for his product. Prices for farm output rose, and his cash receipts rose as well; in fact, they more than doubled. But when European farms resumed their output following the war, the American farmers' crops simply glutted the market. Although prices fell precipitously (40 per cent in the single year 1920–1921), the purchases of farm products did not respond in anything like equal measure. As a result, the cash receipts of the farmer toppled almost as fast as prices. Meanwhile, his taxes were up by some 70 per cent, and his mortgage payments and his cost of living in general had approximately doubled.

There is a lesson here in theory as well as history. Had farmers constituted an oligopolistic market, the decline in farm income might have been limited. A few producers, facing an inelastic demand for their products, can see the sense in mutually curtailing output. Rather than flooding a market which does not want their product, they can agree, tacitly or otherwise, to hold back production to some amount which the market will absorb at a reasonable price. But the individual farmer is about as far from an oligopolist as one can imagine. When the price for his crop falls, it gains the individual farmer nothing to decrease his output. On the contrary, in his highly competitive situation, the best that he can do is to rush to sell as much as he can before things get worse—thereby unwittingly *making* things worse.

At its core, the trouble with the farm sector was that the market mechanism in this particular case did not yield a satisfactory result.[3] That might not have been so serious, had it not been for another development: while agriculture remained static and stagnant, the manufacturing sector was growing by leaps and bounds. Yet its growth was undermined because a fifth of the nation—the agricultural sector—

---

[3] In theory, we will remember, there was a cure for situations in which the producers of one commodity were undercompensated relative to other pursuits: producers would leave the undercompensated field for more lucrative occupations. Indeed, the American farmer tried this cure. It has been estimated that twenty farmers left the soil to seek city work for every urban worker who came to the land. Unfortunately, the cure did not work fast enough. While the agricultural sector steadily diminished in relative size, it could not shrink its absolute numbers significantly. From 1910 to 1930 approximately 10 million farmers remained "locked" on the farm, perhaps half of them barely contributing to national output beyond their own meager livelihoods.

was unable to match the growing volume of production with a growing volume of purchasing power. As the farmers' buying power lagged, it pulled down the demand for tractors, cars, gasoline and electric motors, and manufactured consumer goods generally. Weakness on the farm was thus symptomatic of a weakness throughout the economy, a failure of purchasing power across the whole lower stratum of the nation to keep up with the tempo of national industrial production.

Weakness in the Factory

Most economists of the 1920's, as we have said, would have agreed that there was a source of potential trouble on the farm. Had we suggested that there might be another potential breeding ground for trouble in the factory or the mine, however, few would have given their assent. Most people's eyes, during the 1920's, were fixed on only one aspect of the industrial sector—production—and here there was surely little reason for complaint.

Yet had scrutiny penetrated a bit deeper, very serious signs might well have been spotted in this presumably most buoyant section of the economy. For while production was steadily rising, *employment* was not. In manufacturing, for example, physical output in 1929 was up 49 per cent over 1920, whilst employment was precisely unchanged. In mining, output was up 43 per cent, while employment had shrunk some 12 per cent. In transportation and in the utility industry again output was higher—slightly in transportation, spectacularly in utility's electrical output—and again employment had actually declined.

Overall employment had not, of course, declined. It was significantly up in construction, in trade and finance, in the service industries and in government. But note that all these employment-absorbing industries were characterized by one common denominator: they were all singularly devoid of technological advance. Or to put it the other way around, all the employment-static or declining industries were singularly characterized by rapid technological advance. Pressing against the overall upward tendency of the economy was an undertow of *technological displacement*.

Heretofore in our frequent consideration of technology, we have never stopped to inquire what its effects might be on employment. Rather, we have implicitly assumed those effects to be positive, as we dwelt on the capacity of industrial technology to increase output. Yet it is not difficult to see that technology need not always be favorable for employment. When a new invention creates a new industry, such as the automobile, it is clear that its employment-creating effect can be enormous. Yet, even in such an instance there is an undertow, albeit a small one, as the growing automobile industry crowds out the old carriage industry. When we turn to inventions which do not create new *demands*, but which merely make an established industry more productive, it is clear that the initial impact of technical change can generate serious unemployment.

How are such technologically displaced workers re-employed? We will return to this question later in our chapter.* At this juncture, we want to examine still further the effect of rapid technological change in the "displacing industries," themselves, during the 1920's. Here we see an interesting fact. As production soared and employment sagged, the output per man-hour rose rapidly; in fact, between 1920 and 1929 it increased over 30 per cent in transportation, over 40 per cent in mining, and over 60 per cent in manufacturing.[4] This much larger flow of production per hour meant that wages could have been raised substantially or prices cut sharply. But this is not what we find to have been the case. Only on the unionized railroads did wage rates rise (by about 5 per cent). In mining, hourly earnings fell by nearly 20 per cent, and in manufacturing they remained steady. Since the hours of work per week were also declining, the average annual earnings of employees in these industries were far from keeping pace with the rise in their productivity. In mining, average yearly earnings fell from $1,700 to $1,481. In transportation and manufacturing, yearly earnings fell from 1920 through 1922 and did not regain 1920 levels until 1928 and 1929.

Thus the gains from higher productivity were not passed along to the industrial worker in terms of higher wages. Were they passed along via lower prices? Yes, to some extent. The overall cost of living between 1920 and 1929 fell by about 15 per cent. Part of this reduction, as we have seen, was due to falling food prices. Non-food goods fell sharply in price from 1920 post-war peaks to 1921; thereafter they, too, declined by about 15 per cent up to 1929, but the fall was not enough to distribute all the gains from industrial technology. How do we know this? Because the *profits* of large manufacturing corporations soared between 1920 and 1929. From 1916 through 1925, profits for these companies

---

* See *The Making of Economic Society*, pp. 176–78.

[4] These productivity indexes cannot be computed from our previous output and employment figures, since weekly hours changed. For the original figures, see *Historical Statistics of the United States*, Series W.

had averaged around $730-odd million a year; from 1926 through 1929, they averaged $1,400 million. Indeed, in the year 1929, profits were triple those of 1920.[5]

The Maldistribution of Income

Now we can generalize from what we have just discovered about the trend of wages and profits, to state one further reason for the sudden weakness which overcame the economy, beginning in 1929. Income was distributed in such a way as to make the system vulnerable to economic shocks.

This does *not* mean that somehow the American economy was failing to generate "enough" purchasing power to buy its own output. An economy always creates enough potential buying power to purchase what it has produced, for behind the price tag of each item of output there is always an equivalent sum of income. We have only to look any corporation income statement to see that all its costs of production have been matched by payments to someone: in part to workers as wages; in part to office help as salaries; in part to executives; in part to other enterprises as payments for raw materials, for rent, for services; in part to shareholders as dividends; in part to "itself" as depreciation accruals and retained profits. There can never be an insufficient creation of aggregate purchasing power, because *every cost is someone's income*.

There can, however, be a very serious *maldistribution* of the income payments arising from production. For not all the proceeds arising from production may be placed in the hands of people who will *exercise* their purchasing power. Incomes paid out to the lower-paid strata of the labor force do, indeed, return to the stream of purchasing power, for the working man tends to spend his wages quickly. But incomes which take the form of profits, or depreciation accruals, or as very high individual compensations may not quickly turn over as purchasing power. Profits or high incomes may be saved. They may eventually return to the great stream of purchasing demand, but income which is saved does not "automatically" return via the route of consumption expenditure. Instead, it must find a different route—the route of investment, of capital-building.

In our next pages we shall be dealing with this central problem. Now, it is enough for us to see how a shift of income distribution to potential savers creates the *possibility* for short-circuit in the economic

---

[5] *Historical Statistics of the United States*, V 236.

flow. Returning to the economy in 1929, we can now see as well what was perhaps the deepest-seated reason for its vulnerability: the fact that its income payments were not going in sufficient volume to those who would surely spend them. We have already understood why farmers and working men, who were indeed possessed of a "limitless" desire to consume, were pinched in their *ability* to buy. Now we must complete the picture by seeing how the failure to distribute the gains of productivity to the lower-income groups swelled the incomes of those who were potential non-spenders.

What we see here is an extraordinary, and steadily worsening, concentration of incomes. By 1929, the 15,000 families or individuals at the apex of the national pyramid, with incomes of $100,000 or more each, probably received as much income as 5 to 6 million families at

Percentage Shares of Total Income Received by the Top 1 per Cent and Top 5 per Cent of the Total Population

	Top 1 per cent	Top 5 per cent
1919	12.2	24.3
1923	13.1	27.1
1929	18.9	33.5

NOTE.—The table shows the "disposable income variant": i.e., income after payment of taxes and receipt of capital gains.
Source: *Historical Statistics of the United States*, G 135–6.

the bottom of the pyramid. There was more involved than just a matter of moral equity. It meant that the prosperity of the twenties—and for the majority of the nation it *was* a prosperity of hitherto unequalled extent—in fact covered over an economic situation of grave potentialities. For *if* the nation's on-going momentum should be checked, in this lopsided distribution of purchasing power lay a serious problem. So long as the high profits and salaries and dividends continued to be returned to the income stream, all was well. But what if they should not be?

Deeper Reasons: The Business Cycle

Why should they not be returned? Why should not the circular flow of production and income go on indefinitely?

The questions once again call to our attention an aspect of the process of economic advance which we have not previously noted. The path of industrial advance, whose main trajectory we have already traced, did not take place in a regular and uninterrupted fashion. Rather, it manifested itself in a curiously uneven path—in periods of more-rapid-than-average advance and periods of slower-than-average advance, which we can trace well back into the nineteenth century.

Note from the chart how uneven is the line of the path of total output. We can trace this unevenness not alone in figures for production, such as we see above, but in the rise and fall of prices and in expansions and contractions of employment.[6] We call this irregular wave-like course *the business cycle.*

Growth of Gross National Product

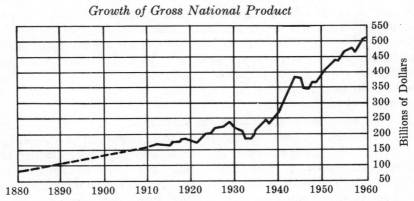

Source: *Economic Growth in the United States* (New York: Committee for Economic Development, 1961).

The business cycle is, in fact, an over-simplification. If we examine business statistics carefully, we can see a number of minor fluctuations as well as larger and bolder ones. Careful students of these fluctuations have discerned at least two basic rhythms of cycles. There is a short cycle which typically measures some two or three years from peak to peak (or from trough to trough). There is a longer cycle, lasting from seven to ten years, from peak to peak or trough to trough. (There is also some evidence of a "long swing" of twenty years from top to top.) Even this by no means exhausts the cycles that can be found by study-

---

[6] This graph shows the swings of gross output *after* regular and predictable seasonal fluctuations (like the seasonal increase of retail sales at Christmastime) have been eliminated.

ing the data of production in various industries. For example, we can discern a fairly regular housing cycle with a seventeen-year duration, a textile industry cycle of about two years, a hog production cycle of three to five years, and a number of others. But usually, when we talk of *the* business cycle, we refer to the big seven- or eight-year swings.

The Critical Role of Capital Formation

What causes these cycles? If we think of them as *variations in the rate of growth*, we already know part of the answer. Since growth is caused by capital formation, these swings in growth must be caused by *swings in the rate of capital formation*. Behind the profile of prosperity and recession lies the critical variable element of expenditure for capital goods. When "times" are good, they are good because we are adding rapidly to our inventories, our stock of machines and equipment, our plant and housing, our public works. When times are bad, we are no longer building up as rapidly our stock of capital goods, private and public.

Why are capital expenditures so unstable?

The reason lies partly in the very nature of capital goods—in their durability, their long economic life. Unlike consumer goods, which tend to be quickly used up—*consumed*—capital goods endure. Their replacement tends to be more irregular than the cycle of consumer replacement. At least *some* consumption activity must always be maintained to sustain life itself, but for a considerable period a society can live off its old capital goods and can defer the day of renewing them.[7]

More important is the fact that *additional* capital goods—the net investment which constitutes the core of economic growth—are similarly subject to a much more irregular pattern of demand than additional consumer goods. Add to a man's income, and you are reasonably certain that he will add to his own consumption. Economists speak of a *propensity to consume*, a dependable tendency to translate higher incomes into at least some additional consumption.

The propensity to invest is a much more uncertain phenomenon. In contrast to consumer goods, capital goods are not bought for per-

---

[7] Obviously there is not an absolutely clear-cut division between all consumer goods and all capital goods. Some consumer goods, like a TV set or a car, are durable, like capital goods, and are called "consumer durables." As we would expect, their purchases are also postponable, and therefore consumer durable sales also exhibit strong cyclical swings. If the exact placement of some goods is occasionally difficult, there is little confusion between the broad categories. A steel plant, a railroad, a hydroelectric dam are very clearly differentiated from food, clothing, or the movies.

sonal use. Nobody consumes a lathe or a blast furnace. These goods are bought because they are expected to yield a *profit* when put to use. Thus we commonly hear it said that a new store, a new machine, or an additional stock of inventory must "pay for itself," and so it must. The additional output that new capital investment makes possible must find a market. *If for any reason a profit is not anticipated, the new investment will not be made.*

The *expectation of profit* (which may be greater or less than profits actually being realized at the moment) plays a crucial role in the rate of capital formation. But why—and this is obviously the key question —should a profit not be anticipated?

There are many possible answers. One of them may be that a speculative collapse, such as the great Crash, destroys "confidence" or impairs financial integrity and leads to a period of retrenchment while financial affairs are put in order. Another reason may be that costs shoot up and monetary troubles impede the boom: the banks may become loaned up and money for new capital projects may suddenly become "tight" and dear. Still another reason may be that consumption expenditures are sluggish, owing perhaps to a maldistribution of income, as in the late 1920's, thereby discouraging plant expansion. Or the rate of population growth or of family formation may decline, bringing a slowdown in the demand for housing. Or the boom may simply die a "natural death"—that is, the wave of technological advance on which it rode may peter out, the great investments needed to build up a tremendous industry may be completed, and no second wave of equal capital-attracting magnitude may immediately rise to take its place.

· · · · · · · · · ·

The Experience of the Great Depression*

Frederick Lewis Allen

Since Hoover's first fever of activity after the Panic, he had been leery of any direct governmental offensive against the Depression. He had preferred to let economic nature take its course. "Economic depression," he insisted, "cannot be cured by legislative action or executive pronouncement. Economic wounds must be healed by the

* Abridgment of pp. 38–39, 53, 63–65, 154–55 from *Since Yesterday* (Harper & Row edition) by Frederick Lewis Allen. Copyright 1939, 1940, by Harper & Row, Publishers, Inc. Reprinted by permission of Harper & Row.

action of the cells of the economic body—the producers and consumers themselves." So he stood aside and waited for the healing process to assert itself, as according to the hallowed principles of laissez-faire economics it should.

But he was not idle meanwhile. For already there was a fierce outcry for federal aid, federal benefits of one sort or another; and in this outcry he saw a grave threat to the federal budget, the self-reliance of the American people, and the tradition of local self-rule and local responsibility for charitable relief. He resolved to defeat this threat. Although he set up a national committee to look after the unemployment relief situation, this committee was not to hand out federal funds; it was simply to co-ordinate and encourage the state and local attempts to provide for the jobless out-of-state appropriations and local charitable drives. (Hoover was quite right, said those well-to-do people who told one another that a "dole" like the one in England would be "soul-destroying.") He hotly opposed the war veterans' claim for a bonus, only to see the Adjusted Compensation Act passed over his veto. He vetoed pension bills. To meet the privation and distress caused by the drought he urged a Red Cross campaign and recommended an appropriation to enable the Department of Agriculture to loan money "for the purpose of seed and feed for animals," but fought against any handouts by the federal government to feed human beings.

In all this Hoover was desperately sincere. He saw himself as the watchdog not only of the Treasury, but of America's "rugged individualism." "This is not an issue," he said in a statement to the press,

as to whether people shall go hungry or cold in the United States. It is solely a question of the best method by which hunger and cold shall be prevented. It is a question as to whether the American people, on one hand, will maintain the spirit of charity and mutual self-help through voluntary giving and the responsibility of local government as distinguished, on the other hand, from appropriations out of the federal Treasury for such purposes.... I have ... spent much of my life in fighting hardship and starvation both abroad and in the southern states. I do not feel that I should be charged with lack of human sympathy for those who suffer, but I recall that in all the organizations with which I have been connected over these many years, the foundation has been to summon the maximum of self-help.... I am willing to pledge myself that if the time should ever come that the voluntary agencies of the country, together with the local and state governments, are unable to find resources with which to prevent hunger and suffering in my country, I will ask the aid of every resource of the federal govern-

ment because I would no more see starvation amongst our country-
men than would any senator or congressman. I have faith in the
American people that such a day will not come.

. . . .

Hoover had tried to keep hands off the economic machinery of
the country, to permit a supposedly flexible system to make its own
adjustments of supply and demand. At two points he had intervened,
to be sure: he had tried to hold up the prices of wheat and cotton,
unsuccessfully; and he had tried to hold up wage-rates, with partial
and temporary success. Otherwise he had mainly stood aside to let
prices and profits and wages follow their natural course. But no natural
adjustment could be reached unless the burdens of debt could also be
naturally reduced through bankruptcies. And in America, as in other
parts of the world, the economic system had now become so complex
and interdependent that the possible consequences of widespread
bankruptcy—to the banks, the insurance companies, the great holding-
company systems, and the multitudes of people dependent upon them—
had become too appalling to contemplate. The theoretically necessary
adjustment became a practically unbearable adjustment. Therefore
Hoover was driven to the point of intervening to protect the debt
structure—first by easing temporarily the pressure of international
debts without canceling them, and second by buttressing the banks
and big corporations with federal funds.

Thus a theoretically flexible economic structure became rigid at a
vital point. The debt burden remained almost undiminished. Bowing
under the weight of debt—and other rigid costs—business thereupon
slowed still further. As it slowed, it discharged workers or put them on
reduced hours, thereby reducing purchasing power and intensifying
the crisis.

It is almost useless to ask whether Hoover was right or wrong.
Probably the method he was driven by circumstances to adopt would
have brought recovery very slowly, if at all, unless devaluation of the
currency had given a fillip to recovery—and devaluation to Hoover
was unthinkable. It is also almost useless to ask whether Hoover was
acting with a tory heartlessness in permitting financial executives to
come to Washington for a corporate dole when men and women on the
edge of starvation were denied a personal dole. What is certain is that
at a time of such widespread suffering no democratic government
could seem to be aiding the financiers and simultaneously seem to be
disregarding the plight of its humbler citizens without losing the
confidence of the public. For the days had passed when men who lost

their jobs could take their working tools elsewhere and contrive an independent living, or cultivate a garden patch and thus keep body and soul together, or go West and begin again on the frontier. When they lost their jobs they were helpless. Desperately they turned for aid to the only agency responsible to them for righting the wrongs done them by a blindly operating economic society: they turned to the government. How could they endorse a government which gave them—for all they could see—not bread, but a stone?

The capitalist system had become so altered that it could not function in its accustomed ways, and the consequences of its failure to function had become too cruel to be borne by free men. Events were marching, and Herbert Hoover was to be among their victims, along with the traditional economic theories of which he was the obstinate and tragic spokesman.

As the second year of the Depression drew to an end and the third one began, a change was taking place in the mood of the American people.

"Depression," as Peter F. Drucker has said, "shows man as a senseless cog in a senselessly whirling machine which is beyond human understanding and has ceased to serve any purpose but its own." The worse the machine behaved, the more were men and women driven to try to understand it. As one by one the supposedly fixed principles of business and economics and government went down in ruins, people who had taken these fixed principles for granted, and had shown little interest in politics except at election time, began to try to educate themselves. For not even the comparatively prosperous could any longer deny that something momentous was happening.

.   .   .   .

Perhaps the worst thing about this Depression was its inexorable continuance year after year. Men who have been sturdy and self-respecting workers can take unemployment without flinching for a few weeks, a few months, even if they have to see their families suffer; but it is different after a year . . . two years . . . three years . . . . Among the miserable creatures curled up on park benches or standing in dreary lines before the soup kitchens in 1932 were men who had been jobless since the end of 1929.

At the very bottom of the economic scale the conditions may perhaps best be suggested by two brief quotations. The first, from Jonathan Norton Leonard's *Three Years Down*, describes the plight of Pennsylvania miners who had been put out of company villages after a blind and hopeless strike in 1931:

Reporters from the more liberal metropolitan papers found thousands of them huddled on the mountainsides, crowded three or four families together in one-room shacks, living on dandelions and wild weed-roots. Half of them were sick, but no local doctor would care for the evicted strikers. All of them were hungry and many were dying of those providential diseases which enable welfare authorities to claim that no one has starved.

The other quotation is from Louise V. Armstrong's *We Too Are the People,* and the scene is Chicago in late spring of 1932:

One vivid, gruesome moment of those dark days we shall never forget. We saw a crowd of some fifty men fighting over a barrel of garbage which had been set outside the back door of a restaurant. American citizens fighting for scraps of food like animals.

Human behavior under unaccustomed conditions is always various. One thinks of the corporation executive to whom was delegated the job of discharging several hundred men: he insisted on seeing every one of them personally and taking an interest in each man's predicament, and at the end of a few months his hair had turned prematurely gray. . . . The Junior League girl who reported with pride a Depression economy: she had cut a piece out of an old fur coat in the attic and bound it to serve as a bathmat. . . . The banker who had been plunged deeply into debt by the collapse of his bank: he got a $30,000 job with another bank, lived on $3,000 a year, and honorably paid $27,000 a year to his creditors. . . . The wealthy family who lost most of their money but announced bravely that they had "solved their Depression problem" by discharging fifteen of their twenty servants, and showed no signs of curiosity as to what would happen to these fifteen. . . . The little knot of corporation officials in a magnificent skyscraper office doctoring the books of the company to dodge bankruptcy. . . . The crowd of Chicago Negroes standing tight-packed before a tenement-house door to prevent the landlord's agents from evicting a neighbor family: as they stood there, hour by hour, they sang hymns. . . . The one-time clerk carefully cutting out pieces of cardboard to put inside his shoes before setting out on his endless job-hunting round, and telling his wife the shoes were now better than ever. . . . The man in the little apartment next door who had given up hunting for jobs, given up all interest, all activity, and sat hour by hour in staring apathy.

.   .   .   .

The Depression had wrecked so many of the assumptions upon which the American people had depended that millions of them were inwardly shaken.

Let us look for a moment at the pile of wreckage. In it we find the assumption that well-favored young men and women, coming out of school or college, could presently get jobs as a matter of course; the assumption that ambition, hard work, loyalty to the firm, and the knack of salesmanship would bring personal success; the assumption that poverty (outside of the farm belt and a few distressed communities) was pretty surely the result of incompetence, ignorance, or very special misfortune, and should be attended to chiefly by local charities; the assumption that one could invest one's savings in "good bonds" and be assured of a stable income thereafter, or invest them in the "blue-chip" stocks of "our leading American corporations" with a dizzying chance of appreciation; the assumption that the big men of Wall Street were economic seers, that business forecasters could forecast, and that business cycles followed nice orderly rhythms; and the assumption that the American economic system was sure of a great and inspiring growth.

Not everybody, of course, had believed all these things. Yet so many people had based upon one or more of them their personal conceptions of their status and function in society that the shock of seeing them go to smash was terrific. Consider what happened to the pride of the business executive who had instinctively valued himself, as a person, by his salary and position—only to see both of them go; to the banker who found that the advice he had been giving for years was made ridiculous by the turn of events, and that the code of conduct he had lived by was now under attack as crooked; to the clerk or laborer who had given his deepest loyalty to "the company"—only to be thrown out on the street; to the family who had saved their pennies, decade after decade, against a "rainy day"—only to see a torrent of rain sweep every penny away; to the housewife whose ideal picture of herself had been of a person who "had nice things" and was giving her children "advantages" economic and social—and who now saw this picture smashed beyond recognition; and to the men and women of all stations in life who had believed that if you were virtuous and industrious you would of course be rewarded with plenty—and who now were driven to the wall. On what could they now rely? In what could they now believe?

Origins of a Welfare State*

Paul K. Conkin

The misery of depression multiplied the need for public welfare. The Democratic sweep in the election of 1934 created a favorable political climate for new federal action. Several New Deal agency heads had already worked out ambitious programs and waited hopefully for funds. Mounting public pressure, often fanned by nostrum-peddling demagogues, helped mute established inhibitions. The [Supreme] Court deathblow to the NRA in 1935, plus congressional pressures, forced Roosevelt to seek a new labor policy, while bitter attacks from a majority of businessmen so angered him that he gladly turned to the working classes for political support. Finally, a growing number of his advisers accepted a monetary, budgetary approach to a still elusive recovery and thus welcomed the deficits involved in large relief programs. These pressures all converged on Congress in 1935, producing a new body of legislation that, with almost unbelievable speed, launched the American welfare state, a brand new, large, ungainly infant, destined to survive all the hazards of childhood and a maladjusted adolescence, eventually to mature in the Great Society, still ugly but increasingly popular.

The term *welfare state* has many connotations, accompanied by degrees of emotional approval or distaste. To a few Americans it is an antonym of *freedom*, a synonym of *socialism*, a repudiation of responsibility, a catalyst of character decline and civilization's rot. To others it connotes halfway, palliative measures, mere sops to the exploited in behalf of preserving privilege and unfair advantage. Rooted in the conservatism of a Bismarck, it is the complete antithesis of socialism. To a much larger group, it is an imperfect but necessary compromise between various contending forces and is thus the middle way, the moderate answer. Despite all the bitterness of the thirties, or even of the sixties, a type of welfare capitalism has become the established system in America, approved by a substantial majority of the voters. It is now conventional and orthodox, however much bolstered by an effective political appeal that still makes it sound progressive and daring, which it really never was.

In a loose way, everyone favors enhancing the general welfare. The problem is one of means. In the American past the key term was always

* From pages 53–67 in *The New Deal*, by Paul K. Conkin. Copyright © 1967 by the Thomas Y. Crowell Company.

opportunity, with a type of disciplined freedom closely connected. Governments had a crucial role—protecting and extending opportunity. In this sense, every good state was a welfare state. In a free society, with beckoning opportunities, with no special privileges, each individual or cooperative effort to take advantage of existing opportunities was conceived as a lesson in responsibility, as an inducement to good character, and as a fulfilling experience. Such a simple but profound faith lay at the moralistic heart of American politics. Private property, meaning the actual means of production, and free enterprise, meaning the private right to manage these means, were indispensable elements in this faith. In fact, they were at the heart of a moral society. Everyone should have an opportunity to own and manage, or at least to share in the owning and management, of productive property. But, to repeat a truism, the faith survived but not the sustaining environment. There was never as much opportunity as the faith presumed. By 1930 only a few people could own and manage property. In this sense opportunity disappeared. But an ersatz type of opportunity—to work for other men, to sell one's labor to those who did own and manage property— replaced an earlier dream of farm or shop, along with an ersatz type of property—common stock, or claims on profits but no real role in management. In the Depression even these poor substitutes paled. Up to fifteen million family heads could find no market for their labor and had to turn either to private or public charity.

This simplified analysis helps clarify the welfare state under Roosevelt and the mixed reception to it. Some welfare measures directed at better opportunity, such as education, had been urged by Jefferson and long since provided by state governments, although Emerson first asked the vital question—opportunity for what, for ownership and enterprise, for responsibility, involvement, and fulfillment, or just opportunity for productive employment. In the New Deal, some legislation, typified by the Farm Tenancy Act of 1937, was directed, realistically or not, at the old Jeffersonian idea of true property and true enterprise, at restored opportunity in the most sweeping sense. This was paralleled by what seemed a considerable, even devastating attack on entrenched privilege, on monopolistic wealth, on concentrated economic power, on unfair rules in the market place. At this point the New Deal was most traditional, not only re-echoing the rhetoric of progressivism but of Puritanism. The idea of broad opportunity, the sense of moral responsibility, was an older and deeper orthodoxy than laissez faire, as such a conventional American, such an able politician, as Roosevelt always sensed. But much of the welfare legislation of the thirties was of a different sort. Simply, it was a "take-care-of" type of welfare. The federal government undertook numerous programs to succor the unemployed, the elderly, and the exploited, by direct relief, by work programs, and by regulative laws that forced employers to be more generous.

The most penetrating criticism of government charity came from Jeffersonians and socialists. To such an old Jeffersonian liberal as Herbert Hoover, the assumption of direct responsibility for the individual by any government, and particularly by a distant federal government, endangered the whole idea of personal responsibility and misconstrued the area of responsibility rightly reserved for government. Sustained gifts from governments would create a passive, alienated group of men, without a real stake in society, with no compelling involvement, and with a dangerous political tendency to march in step with any demagogue promising more welfare. He always insisted that the long-range welfare of the individual could only be served by his active, creative participation in our private economy, and not by accepting some dole, concealed or not. Thus welfare was a dangerous answer to depression; recovery and restored opportunity the only legitimate, long-term answer.

On the socialist left, the most astute critics agreed. But, unlike Hoover they did not expect to solve the problems of depression by restoring the business society of the twenties. They felt that welfare measures obscured the continued injustices of capitalism, thus allaying the rightful demands for economic justice. Welfare, by stilling the voice of dissent, and by stimulating consumption and higher profits, represented a type of government insurance for a capitalist economy. Even if there were some leveling of wealth, some truly progressive taxes, there could be no true opportunity. Instead of aid to the unemployed, the existing economic system should be replaced by one that not only guaranteed employment but that gave to all citizens some sense of personal involvement and some share in ownership and management. These socialists, whether Christians, Marxists, or pragmatists, still had the vision of a cooperative commonwealth.

But the battle over welfare legislation, then or now, usually did not revolve around fundamental issues. On one level the advocacy or opposition was framed in light of immediate economic interest. This included both those who asked, "What can I get?" as well as those who cried, "What will it cost me?" The battle of interests was clothed in the folklore of our society, in the myths accepted by millions of people. Thus, the verbal icons of Jefferson were wrapped tightly around the most unpalatable injustices and the most transparent privileges. The old cliches of populism and progressivism, stripped of their real meanings, were used to oversimplify the very complexities that demanded thought and laborious action.

The welfare legislation of 1935, or the second hundred days, has occasioned critical divergence among historians. Raymond Moley first condemned Roosevelt for deserting a true concert of interests and for discontinuing early cooperative overtures to business. To him, the new welfare measures, joined with the class appeals in the campaign of 1936, represented a demagogic radicalism and a betrayal of all Roosevelt's early promises. In a loose way, most other historians, including textbook authors, have accepted Moley's contention that Roosevelt moved to the "left" in 1935, but, often reflecting a lingering progressive bias, they have usually approved of the shift. [Rexford G.] Tugwell reversed the judgment, as had contemporary socialist critics. He agreed with Moley that Roosevelt had gone progressive, probably for political rather than ideological reasons. But he denied that it was a legitimate turn to the left, condemning it as a conservative (i.e., progressive) betrayal of the concert of interests, which he defined in terms of planning rather than of Moley's partnership with business. For Tugwell, the old progressive rhetoric, however radical it sounded, was only political nonsense employed to disguise the return of America to private manipulators. [Arthur] Schlesinger, with some sympathy for Tugwell's position, sympathized with the more practical expedients pursued by Roosevelt and his new, Brandeisian advisers. He thus described the New Deal as moving to the left politically, economically to the right of Tugwell's planning concepts, but not necessarily to the right of early New Deal programs.

The largest welfare program of the New Deal, and of American history, began in 1935. A newly elected, exceedingly generous Congress approved a $4.88 billion Emergency Relief Appropriation, to be spent as Roosevelt saw fit. This was, up until this time, the largest appropriation in American history and the largest accretion to the national debt. It was used to consolidate and expand numerous early, temporary relief programs, which had served up to 30 million people. About $1.5 billion, the largest single block, went to Harry Hopkins and to a new relief organization created by executive order, the huge Works Progress Administration (WPA). In turn, the WPA used most of its share, plus endless new appropriations, for work programs for the unemployed. At times its projects resembled those of the more reputable PWA [Public Works Administration], even as a favored Hopkins cut into what [Harold] Ickes believed should have been his share of the appropriation. Against the wishes of congressional liberals, WPA wages were generally scaled below those of private industry, and anyone offered private employment became ineligible for WPA work. Burdened by a lack of developed plans for massive public works, by an over-supply of unskilled laborers, and by rigid rules, the WPA was inefficient by any private standard. Nonetheless, the completed projects in part compensated for the money spent and represented a great gain over direct doles. Despite vigorous efforts to maintain high morale, and despite the sincere appreciation of most workers, the WPA could not escape some of the stigma of relief. In fact, derisive opponents would not let it. Also, the WPA could only employ about a third of those who needed work, leaving millions to the care or neglect of states. Many had to remain on a dole, often supplemented by free food distributed by a Federal Surplus Commodities Corporation.

Less expensive and more daring were the several white collar programs set up by the WPA, drawing upon earlier experiences of the CWA [Civil Works Administration] and some state relief administrations. For the first time in American history, the federal government gave a vast subsidy to some of the fine arts and to scholarship (Federal Theater, Federal Writers', and Federal Art projects). Much of the art, particularly plays, sculpture, and painting, reflected the social concern of the thirties. The most rewarding aspect of these programs was the degree of participation. Music, painting, and the theater, usually frivolous sideshows of the wealthy, centered in a few large cities and priced beyond the common people, were now merged with daily life, in murals on public buildings, in local symphonies, in amateur theaters. Just as important, thousands of people were able to participate in creative endeavors, including handicrafts. Another subagency, the National Youth Administration, directed by Hopkins' assistant, Aubrey Williams, inaugurated a vast scholarship program under the guise of student work, and set up work projects for school dropouts.

A second large block of the relief appropriation went to Rexford G. Tugwell, who headed another new agency, the Resettlement Administration (RA). It absorbed the rural relief and rehabilitation programs of the old Federal Emergency Relief Administration and the uncompleted communities of the Division of Subsistence Homesteads. Tugwell had more plans than funds. As the title suggests, he wanted to resettle urban slum dwellers in autonomous garden cities and submarginal farmers in new, productive farm villages, with cooperation a guiding concern of both groups. His greatest monuments were three suburban greenbelt cities and a few dozen new farm communities. The largest share of his funds had to be used to continue a rural relief program. One of the liberals disillusioned with the failure of the Agricultural Adjustment Administration to become an instrument of rural reform, and long contemptuous of the Extension Service, Tugwell set up a duplicate farm organization, with its own agents, but dedicated only to the exploited and underprivileged.

The RA would not compromise with existing evils. Almost alone, it fought for equal benefits for Negroes. It was the only New Deal agency to set up group medical plans. Contrary to the idols of Congress and to the ruling commitment of the Department of Agriculture, RA leaders questioned fee simple [outright] ownership and experimented both with long-term leases and co-operative farms. Concerned with farm labor, it set up migratory camps and tried to alleviate the plight of the "Okies." But in most cases it loaned funds to small farmers for needed equipment or vital necessities and then supervised their farm program, protected them from exploitation, and took a percentage of their crops as repayment. The RA became a new, solicitous bank for small landowners and a second, protective landlord for tenants. It was not only one of the most honest but probably the most class-conscious of New Deal agencies. Soon it antagonized practically every vested interest, a good mark of its relative effectiveness. Yet its funds permitted it only to touch the problems of rural areas, particularly in the South. With restricted prerogatives, plus a tenant-purchase program at odds with its earlier orientation, the RA moved into the Department of Agriculture in 1937 and became the Farm Security Administration (FSA). Congress gleefully destroyed it during the war, replacing it with an attentuated Farmers' Home Administration.

The Social Security Act of 1935 became the supreme symbol of a welfare state. As enacted, it hardly deserved the honor or opprobrium. At most, it set some enduring precedents and established a new area of federal responsibility. As shown by Edwin E. Witte,[1] the bill was tremendously complex, compromising many divergent plans and establishing an array of welfare programs. Although not responsible for the details of the act, Roosevelt had worked for better old age benefits and for unemployment insurance while governor of New York. As early as 1934 he signed a Railroad Retirement Act. In the same year, he witnessed the growing frustration of the underprivileged classes, who had so far reaped a bitter pill in New Deal recovery programs.

---

[1] *Development of the Social Security Act* (Madison: University of Wisconsin Press, 1962).

With unfulfilled expectations, revolutionary feelings grew even faster than in 1932. Various movements, often roughly but arbitrarily classed to the right and left, gained vast public support. Two of these, led by Huey Long and Francis E. Townsend, focused on the extremes of wealth in America and proffered schemes for either sharing the wealth (Long) or providing elaborate pensions for the elderly (Townsend). Naive or oversimplified, their platforms revivified the old problem of Henry George—great wealth and great poverty. Roosevelt, as a good politician, saw the tremendous political appeal of legislation directed at the elderly and unemployed and thus joined his support to that of congressional authors. Even most Republicans, with apprehensive glances over their left shoulders and aware of the mildness of the final version, supported the bill.

The Social Security Act set up the present compulsory tax for retirement benefits, a tax assessed in equal parts on employer and employee. About half of the people were excluded by the original act, including farmers, domestics, and the elderly. The employee tax represented a significant drain from already low payrolls and thus a further obstacle to recovery. The original act did not protect against accidents and illness before retirement, provided no medical insurance, and paid benefits on the basis of past earning instead of present needs. Thus, it was close to a compulsory insurance system, paid for largely by those who benefited. The unemployment insurance provision delegated most responsibility to the states and invited chaotic variations in always inadequate payments. Since the retirement coverage was so limited, the act provided matching federal funds for traditional state pensions for the aged and funds for dependent mothers, children, and the crippled and blind. The present public welfare system, although administered locally and almost always inadequate, is closely tied to this federal assistance.

In housing, as in retirement, the New Deal made a modest, even parsimonious, beginning. The PWA could loan funds to local, limited-dividend housing corporations, for both housing projects and slum clearance. Under Ickes' watchful eyes, only a few projects were approved (less than 25,000 housing units by 1937). The several community programs involved only limited numbers but, in the case of the greenbelt towns of the Resettlement Administration, quite imaginative experiments, not only in housing but in community planning. But there was no follow-up. Instead, beginning in 1934 the government tried to stimulate private construction, aid home buyers, and protect mortgage bankers through a loan insurance program administered by a Federal Housing Administration (FHA). Since the FHA assumed final responsibility for repayment (a service paid for by a tax on borrowers) and required certain standards in construction, this program helped many middle-income families buy homes at a low rate of interest. In no sense was it a federal housing program. In the thirties it did not appreciably stimulate private home building and thus failed as a recovery measure. Finally, in 1937, after years of effort by housing and urban renewal proponents, and particularly by Senator Robert F. Wagner of New York, Roosevelt agreed to support a small housing and slum-clearance program. The Wagner–Steagall Act established the United States Housing Authority as a government corporation. It had $500 million to lend to state or local housing authorities. The terms were generous, with low interest and extended (sixty years) repayments. When housing projects replaced slums, annual contributions by the USHA further subsidized the program. Federal rules required rents well below competitive rates and limited residency to low-income families. The first results, under local direction, were almost universally ugly and depressing developments, segregated, stigmatized by origin and by residency requirements, resented by local citizens, and located in the worst sections of town.

Relief, unemployment insurance, and low-income housing all represented tangible, if limited, benefits for the working class. Roosevelt wanted to help farmers and laborers gain minimal economic security as part of their American birthright. He did not easily move beyond this commitment. Paternal business, if paternal enough, seemed adequate. Early in his presidency, he easily cooperated with businessmen who shared his humane concern and in several cases sided with business in labor–management disputes. Thus, until 1935 he was clearly pro-agriculture, even pro-labor, but not pro-union. But events pushed him into the camp of the labor unions. Section 7(a) of the National Industrial Recovery Act, if liberally interpreted, was indeed the long-awaited Magna Carta of organized labor. In part frustrated by company unions, never given adequate protection by the National Recovery Administration staff, the American Federation of Labor nonetheless acted as if it were a Magna Carta and began large organizational drives. In 1934, strikes erupted throughout the country, often directed by labor radicals rather than by the conservative AFL. From the impetus of the strikes came the revolutionary rise of industrial unions, the schism of 1935, and the vitality and political effectiveness of the new Congress of Industrial Organizations. Militant unionism had its golden age in the thirties. As a whole, union workers loved and supported Roosevelt, while business leaders reviled him. With the death of NRA, Roosevelt had to choose a new labor policy. He belatedly chose the side of the unions. They had votes and loved a Roosevelt willing to show some interest in their problems.*

If 7(a) was the Magna Carta, the National Labor Relations Act of 1935 (Wagner Act) was the Bill of Rights for unions. It involved an almost unbelievable capitulation by the government. The architect of the bill, Senator Wagner, served as chairman of the National Labor Board under the NRA. Frustrated by the business-oriented leadership of Hugh Johnson, the Board had limited success in protecting workers. In 1934 Roosevelt established a National Labor Relations Board (NLRB) as a separate, but rather futile, agency which still had to utilize the statutory provisions of the NIRA. As a result, Wagner fought, without Roosevelt's blessings, for new statutory authority and a new, more powerful NLRB. His bill passed the Senate without Administration support, and then with it breezed through the House. The bill guaranteed the right of collective bargaining by a union chosen by a majority of employees, legalized collective action (strikes, boycotts), and by a code of fair practices outlawed such traditional weapons as the company union, blacklist, and yellow-dog contract. The act empowered a new NLRB to conduct representation elections and hear any complaints from unions. Big labor, in one sweep, almost gained equality with big business. But for the majority of workers, as yet unorganized, the Wagner Act was less important than Social Security. Tied to the interstate commerce clause, it did not protect the bargaining rights of public employees, service and agricultural workers, and workers in strictly intrastate commerce.

The welfare legislation, large in hopes generated, often pitifully small in actual benefits, hardly represented a social revolution. Except for relief, only a small burden had been added to the national budget, and none of the welfare programs significantly redistributed the wealth of the country. Not only Huey Long, but politicians of varied persuasions wanted to lessen disparities of income and accumulated wealth. Some progressives, led by Brandeis and like foes of centralized power, also wanted to help restore competition by placing a tax burden on bigness. Roosevelt, enraged by hostile newspapers and by business criticism, increasingly advised by Felix Frankfurter (then at the Harvard Law School and a Brandeis disciple), and always thirsting for a good fight, presented Congress with a new and biting tax proposal

* For more detailed discussion of the progress of labor in the New Deal, see *Ferment in Labor* by Jerome Wolf, another Insight Series book.

in the spring of 1935. It had two purposes: a fairer sharing of the tax burden and penalties on large enterprise. The bill, soon labeled a "soak-the-rich" measure, provoked an embittered controversy. It marked the most decisive turn by Roosevelt from consensus politics to a clear appeal to the disinherited. The tax message rested on the depressing fact that, so far, New Deal policies had created a more regressive tax system, with greater burdens on consumption and low incomes than on large incomes. Large corporations had used the depression to reduce debts and to increase their liquid capital, even while suffering operating losses, suspending dividends, and thus avoiding taxes. Also, then as now, large incomes escaped existing tax schedules by loopholes and avoidance.

Roosevelt asked for a graduated corporate income tax, a separate intercorporate dividend tax to prevent an escape via subsidiary companies, an inheritance and gift tax, and a more sharply graduated income tax. His message to Congress was loaded with encomium for small enterprise and diatribes against business concentration and large accumulations of wealth. In Congress, Roosevelt, who never pushed the tax bill as strenuously as other legislation, suffered a mild defeat. Only a token corporate income tax passed. The inheritance tax was dropped. In all, small tax increases produced only $250 million in annual revenue. The bill neither soaked the rich, penalized bigness, or significantly helped balance the budget. A later (1936) tax on undistributed dividends and excess profits was likewise attenuated and subsequently repealed. Thus, tax policy was not to play an important role in New Deal economic policy, at least beyond the realm of rhetoric and psychological warfare.

But the battle against bigness became a standard New Deal brand. Not that it ever achieved significant results. That was impossible. The emphasis shifted only after the demise of the NRA. In crucial industries like coal, petroleum, and the retail trades, with many small producers, the federal government almost of necessity continued an NRA type of detailed regulation and protection under new, more carefully drafted legislation. In industries dominated by a few large producers, the collusion and accommodation once again became a private, in part clandestine operation, while Roosevelt's avowed policy was free competition, the prosecution of monopoly, and concessions to small business. Under Thurman Arnold, beginning in 1938, the Antitrust Division of the Department of Justice expanded its operations to the highest level in history, perhaps as much for punitive reasons as for restored competition or, as even Arnold suggested, as a type of folk ritual that at least pointed to the ultimate superiority of government over the corporations.

The most vulnerable area of chaotic and wasteful bigness was in the electrical utilities, where operating companies were often controlled by pyramiding holding companies. In the wake of the Tennessee Valley Authority battles, there were identified political devils. With some glee, Roosevelt asked Congress to pass a Public Utilities Holding Company Act, which would empower the Securities and Exchange Commission to simplify and rationalize the holding companies to make geographic and economic sense and to abolish those without economic justification (the "death sentence"). It also authorized the Federal Power Commission to integrate, under federal controls, operating companies into regional systems. All hell broke loose. Led by able apologists like Wendell Willkie, and by less ethical lobbyists by the hundreds, the utility companies spent a billion dollars to defeat or emasculate the bill. As its first direct slap at Roosevelt, Congress amended the death sentence amid turbulent accusations of unfair lobbying and unfair Administration pressure, both true.

The private utilities won a minor battle, not a war. They still faced severe regulation. Also, in line with TVA, the Administration added vast public power projects at Grand Coulee and Hoover dams and tried for years to get additional valley authorities. In 1935, under the Emergency Relief Appropriation, Roosevelt set up a Rural Electrification Administration (REA) which could not construct rural power facilities but which used low-interest loans in an unsuccessful attempt to encourage private companies to serve rural areas. In 1936 Congress made the REA into an independent lending agency, against a last, vengeful outpouring of vituperation from private power companies. The REA provided low-interest loans to rural cooperatives, which built their own lines and either manufactured or purchased their own power. It became one of the most successful of New Deal agencies, providing not only low-cost power to remote areas but valuable lessons in cooperation and local democracy.

.   .   .   .

The Contribution of Keynes*

Stephen K. Bailey

There are few who would question the contribution of John Maynard Keynes to the theoretical underpinnings of the Full Employment Bill [which, as it was passed in 1946, provided for expanded economic planning]. Care should be taken, however, in assigning his proper historical role. Keynes was not the inspired prophet of a new mystical theology. He was the great verbalizer and rationalizer of a theoretical attitude which was being forced, by the cold facts of the Depression experience, upon a number of European and American economists. In the discussion which follows it should be appreciated that the name of Keynes is being used as a symbol for an intellectual movement. This movement is personalized for reasons of stylistic simplicity. Any other approach would necessitate an impossibly complicated delineation of economic theory and policy from [Thomas] Malthus through men like [Thorstein] Veblen and J. A. Hobson to the articles, reviews, books, and experiences which "pre-Keynesed" Keynes during the twenties and thirties.

. . . .

Keynes's *General Theory of Employment, Interest, and Money*

Keynes's *General Theory* [1936], one of the great watersheds in the history of economic thought, was an attack upon the basic concept of *classical* and *neo-classical* economic thought that the free market capitalistic economy was a self-adjusting mechanism which tended to produce a condition of full employment and a maximum utilization of economic resources. Unemployment, to the classicist, was due to rigidities and imperfections in a system which subsumed perfect competition, perfect mobility of labor and capital, and perfect knowledge on the part of decision-makers. Saving was a major economic virtue, since all savings tended to be invested in the development of new capital goods, which in turn brought employment and increased productivity. The possibility of unutilized savings was discounted since it was believed that, given a tendency in that direction, the interest rate would fall, and a low rate of interest would stimulate further investment. It would also encourage consumer spending, which would in turn stimulate business expansion. Conversely, if savings tended to fall in relation to the demand for investment capital, the rate of interest

---

* Reprinted by permission from Stephen K. Bailey, *Congress Makes a Law* (New York: Columbia University Press, 1950), pp. 14, 15–20.

would rise, coaxing a greater proportion of income into savings. It was a neat theory, but to many it seemed hardly adequate to meet the demonstrated facts of life in the Britain of the twenties and thirties, and the America of the thirties, where, theory or no theory, a vast amount of involuntary unemployment existed and the economic system showed few signs of moving automatically toward the full utilization of resources.

One of the most adequate short analyses of Keynesian theory has been made by Sir William Beveridge (now Lord Beveridge) in his book *Full Employment in a Free Society*.[1]

> The gist of the new approach to the problem of employment... can be put shortly. Employment depends on spending, which is of two kinds—for consumption and for investment; what people spend on consumption gives employment. What they save, i.e. do not spend on consumption, gives employment only if it is invested, which means not the buying of bonds or shares, but expenditure in adding to capital equipment, such as factories, machinery, or ships, or in increasing stocks of raw material. There is not in the unplanned market economy anything that automatically keeps the total spending of both kinds at the point of full employment, that is to say, high enough to employ all the available labour. Adequate total demand for labour in an unplanned market economy cannot be taken for granted.
>
> According to the Keynesian analysis, the possibility of prolonged mass unemployment lies in the fact that decisions to save and decisions to invest are made by different sets of people at different times and for different reasons and thus may get out of step. The amount which any community will try to save is governed, not primarily by the outlets for saving, i.e. the opportunities for investment, but by the total income of the community and its distribution; broadly speaking, if incomes are evenly distributed, less will be saved out of the total than if they are unevenly distributed. The amount which any community will seek to invest is governed, not primarily by the amount of savings available for investment, but by expectation of profits. Savings and investment do not start with any initial tendency to march in step and there is no automatic painless way of keeping them in step or bringing them together if they fall out. The rate of interest, which was supposed to serve this purpose, of regulating automatically the processes of saving and investment, fails to do so. If savings are tending to outrun invest-

---

[1] (New York: W. W. Norton, Inc., 1945), pp. 93–95.

ment, the rate of interest will fall only after a severe decline in the national income....

The argument, it will be seen, is not that the savings of a community in total can outrun the investment. In the sense in which these terms are used in the Keynesian analysis the total savings that a community is, in fact, able to make, can never exceed the total invested; if a number of individuals in the community together try to save more than is being invested, the income of other members of the community will be correspondingly reduced; their losses in poverty and unemployment, their spending of former savings or running into debt will cancel out some of the savings of others and will thus reduce the total savings of the community to that which can be spent in investment....

The Keynesian analysis attacks directly and destroys one of the economic harmonies between savings and investment through the rate of interest, which according to the older theory were assumed to keep the free capitalist system in prosperous equilibrium, with the demand for labour painlessly adjusted to the supply of labour. It destroys incidentally another of these harmonies also—the assumption made by Professor Pigou in 1913 that wage rates could be so adjusted as to abolish unemployment completely, and the inference that in any given situation employment could be increased directly by a general reduction of money wages.

In the shortest possible compass, the Keynesian analysis added up to a reminder that if people stop consuming and stop investing, national income, which according to the Keynesian formula is the sum of consumption and investment, is bound to fall; that the only way to increase national income is by means of increasing either consumption expenditures or investment expenditures or both, and finally, that there are governmental means of doing this in case private enterprise by itself cannot or will not do it.

The Impact of Keynes on American Thinking

Keynes's *General Theory* was published in 1936 and gained currency in America just as the recession of 1937 was in the process of undermining the government's belief that the economy would permanently recover on the basis of a few intravenous injections of purchasing power. To many American economists in and out of the government, Keynes's analysis provided a theoretical summation of the reasons for the failure of the American economy to recover from the Depression. Suddenly everything was clear: an economic plateau had been reached in the United States far below the level of full employment; there was no automatic mechanism within the system which would tend to produce the maximum utilization of resources; full employment could not be reached, consequently, unless the government undertook positive measures on a continuous basis.

With this analysis in mind, American economists and other policy planners began to re-evaluate the New Deal program and to search for the underlying causes of the economic stagnation. The redistribution of income through steeply graduated income taxes, inheritance taxes, and undistributed profits taxes, came to be recognized, not simply as a matter of social justice, but as a positive economic good—since, as Keynes had pointed out, high-income groups save proportionately more (and consequently spend proportionately less) of their income than low-income groups. The 1937 recession came to be explained on the basis, not that government spending had failed, but that it had not been tried on sufficient scale. Budget-balancing as a goal came to be discredited, and a vast literature began to grow around the idea that public borrowing for the purpose of increasing investment and consumption would so raise the national income that the increasing debt burden could be carried with relative ease. Monopolistic elements in the industrial structure came to be viewed in the light of the impact of monopoly upon the rate of saving. As one economist has put it, "a regime of monopoly means high profits which tend to be hoarded; a regime of competition means lower profits which tend to be employed."[2]

All the New Deal attempts to raise purchasing power, promote public works, and foster the development of natural resources came to be endorsed, not just as necessary depression expedients, but as part of an inclusive long-term program of government investment, expenditure, and control, based upon the Keynesian analysis.

In defense of the reason that private enterprise could not take care of idle savings on its own and thereby obviate the necessity of all this government activity, the American Keynesians built up what has come to be called the *maturity* thesis. One lucid statement reads as follows:

> We reach the conclusion that the expansion of the nineteenth and early twentieth centuries was based on building for the future, which carried with it an adequate demand for consumable goods

[2] Moses Abramovitz, "Savings and Investment: Profits vs. Prosperity?" *The American Economic Review*, Part II [Supplement (June, 1942)], 88.

and services in the present. Building for the future was good business in an expanding economic universe with a rapidly growing
population. When the limits of expansion had been reached, when
the rate of population growth slowed down, building for the future
became an increasingly hazardous adventure. Its volume contracted
and with it the ability to buy in the present. Expansion fed upon
itself in the past; contraction feeds upon itself in the present.
These are the basic changes which underlie the reversal of trend
from 1929 to the present. [3]

The Opposition

The analysis of the American Keynesians met with stout opposition
from businessmen and from non-Keynesian economists. And of course
there developed hot intramural fights within the Keynesian fraternity
itself. The business community in general called the *maturity* thesis
ridiculous, classifying it as old and discredited hogwash, and claiming
that the economic stagnation about which the Keynesians talked, was
purely and simply the result of unsettling and hostile New Deal
policies. A let-up on "soak-the-rich" taxes, a decrease in federal expenditures, a reduction in the national debt, a curtailing of the
"irresponsible" power of organized labor and other measures favorable
to business confidence, would, they claimed, open the road to business
expansion, full employment, and general prosperity.

The Depression experience, and Mr. Keynes, set off a long debate
which has by no means ended. The impact of Keynesian thinking on
federal policies was only slightly, even if clearly, noticeable prior to
the war, but its influence on the post-war-employment planning which
developed during the war, was, as we shall see, enormous. Although
the major exponent and modifier of Keynesian theory as applied to
American problems was Professor Alvin Hansen of Harvard, hundreds
of economists and government policy planners had come by the end
of the thirties to accept the Keynesian analysis as the new orthodoxy.
Like most disciples, they sometimes misunderstood and frequently
reinterpreted the master, but they paid him homage even in their
defections. In spite of, and perhaps, on occasion, because of, the general
hostility of the business world to the analyses and projected programs
of American Keynesians, the influence of the latter continued to grow.

---

[3] Seven Harvard and Tufts Economists, *An Economic Program for American
Democracy* (New York: Vanguard Press, 1938), p. 22.

Chapter Three

The Welfare Consensus

From the inception of the New Deal program in the thirties to the present, the federal government has broadened the scope of its involvement in social welfare. The administrations of Harry S. Truman, Dwight D. Eisenhower, and John F. Kennedy saw the expansion of benefits originally provided for in legislation passed during the New Deal period. The Johnson Administration initiated the only substantive change in federal welfare with the passage in 1966 of the Medicare program of medical aid for the aged.

The following is a summary of benefits provided by current welfare legislation. Some of these programs are administered directly by federal agencies, while others are administered by local and state agencies with varying degrees of participation by federal agencies and funds.

Aid for the Aged and Disabled

—The Social Security System, providing pensions for older persons as well as payments to the totally and permanently disabled

—Old-age assistance, providing pensions for those who do not qualify for Social Security benefits

—Medicare

—Aid to the blind, the crippled, and those permanently disabled by disease

—Workmen's compensation, which guarantees either lump sums or monthly payments for people injured on jobs covered by this program

Aid for Children

—Aid for the dependent children of the blind, disabled, and unemployed; aid to children deprived of the support of one or both parents through death, desertion, or imprisonment, where full support is not otherwise available.

—Maternity and child health services, including free public clinics, vaccination programs, school health programs, and other public health measures.

—The school lunch program.

Aid for the Needy

—Unemployment compensation, for people who are discharged through no fault of their own and who are able and willing to work.

—General welfare, for people not covered by unemployment or workmen's compensation who can't meet their minimum needs.

—Federal disaster relief aid for counties of states hit by natural disasters.

—Public works programs for the jobless.

Related Programs

—Veteran's Administration pensions, hospitals, rehabilitation programs.

—Aid to students through fellowships and loans under the National Defense Education Act, and the Education Act of 1963.

—Public housing projects.

This, then, is the broad structure of federal welfare in the 1960's. It is a structure which is accepted today as necessary to our society by most groups. There has recently been little dissent about either the ideology which underlies the program of social welfare, or the design of individual measures. The three selections in this chapter serve to point up the general consensus about welfare in the United States.

A speech by Dwight D. Eisenhower, made in 1952 during his first presidential candidacy, offers insight into the nature of this consensus. Even during this early period when Eisenhower was identified with the conservative wing of the Republican Party, he was not quite ready to condemn welfare legislation as a whole, although he was strongly opposed to such New Deal measures as the Tennessee Valley Authority, federal deficit spending, and broad government participation in the economy. He proposed to bring government back into its supposed "rightful" position vis-a-vis the states and business. This position he called "The Middle Road."

But within a short time after assuming the presidency, Eisenhower changed his position. Confronted by the several recessions of the 1950's, the dependency of the economy on welfare programs such as Social Security, and the existence of heavy Democratic majorities in Congress (which represented a national commitment to welfare spending), Eisenhower was induced to alter his attitudes. Toward the end of his time in office, he reluctantly came to accept welfare capitalism and, in fact, increased many benefits provided under existing welfare statutes. By doing so, Eisenhower incurred the wrath of the far right, but he confirmed the consensus about welfare.

The speech by John F. Kennedy states more explicitly and positively than Eisenhower's the importance of federal welfare to the national well-being.

The excerpt by Professor Reo M. Christenson, "The Logic of the Welfare State," presents the common-sense ideology that lies behind that consensus.

The Middle Road (1952)*

Dwight D. Eisenhower

. . . There are many people in our country who say there are only two roads to the future—one off to the right, following which we become reactionaries. We go back to the place where we think we should have lived in 1852. Then there are others who say you must continually go to the left. Those people say "let the government do it—turn it over to Washington." They go so far to the left that we call them radicals.

A strange thing about these two roads, ladies and gentlemen. As you go further and further to the right, there is less and less concern for the individual. As we pursue this policy to its extreme, we have a laissez-faire [government], and finally a resentful people become so powerful in their distrust of the government that government must use compulsion to force its will upon them and we have tyranny.

Now, let's go to the left. And the government does more and more of the things that are to be done, as it takes your property and compels you to work on it, whether it be on the farm or factory or whatever. It, too, finds it must use compulsion and ends up in tyranny.

The great problem of America today is to take that straight road down the middle, the path of progress that will never allow tyranny to become the feature of American government.

Let's take one or two examples of this application of this middle way. During the Civil War Lincoln had passed a Homestead Law. These great lands of the West were at stake and there were many greedy interests in Washington who wanted these lands turned over to the great combinations or rich men so they could hold them forever in their own right.

---

* This speech was delivered by the Republican presidential candidate in Boise, Idaho, on August 20, 1952.

And there were other groups that said, "Oh, no, the federal government will always keep title to these lands and we will keep title to their surface and everything under them."

But Lincoln had passed a Homestead Law to put that land in the hands of the people, demonstrating his faith not only in the people but in this middle road which led to the progress, the results of which we see today, a beautiful city like Boise sitting in the midst of these mountains.

At the beginning of this century there was such a great concentration of power in such a few combinations, most of them centered in Wall Street, that we had what we call trusts. Now, Theodore Roosevelt set about to break them up. Now, he didn't try to destroy them; he didn't try to destroy the property and the facilities and all of the organization they set up. Neither did he give way to all the proposals made to him to let the government take over.

No, he said, we will simply make them each conform to our laws by breaking them up to the extent they cannot exert undue influence and power over the people of the United States. He chose the middle way and we will remember him forever because of that.

Now, ladies and gentlemen, this middle way today starts off with certain very definite assumptions. It assumes that all Americans of all parties have now accepted and will forever support what we call social gains, the security that people are entitled to in their old age and to make certain they are adequately cared for, insurance against unemployment, equal opportunities for everybody regardless of race, religion, where he was born or what is his national origin.

We have accepted a moral obligation—the education of our young, decent housing, the rights of working men and working women to be productive, the rights of each of us to earn what he can and to save it as far as taxes will let him. We accept as a part of these social gains the fact that Americans must have adequate insurance against disaster.

No one counts that thing a political issue any more. That is part of America. But all of those things, ladies and gentlemen, we call security measures and social gains. They are not goals, they are what America is going to win.

Let's call all those things just a solid floor that keeps all of us from falling into the pit of disaster. But on top of that floor, let's not interfere with the incentive, the ambition, the right of any of you to build the most glorious structure on top of that floor that you can imagine. That is what we want America to be—the product of 156 million people, their incentives, their ambitions, their efforts and their work, and their intelligence translated into accomplishment for the good of all of us.

We have a great program in development not only for ourselves and the betterment of our lives. But each day, ladies and gentlemen, there are 6,000 more Americans than there were the day before. We have got to continue expanding and we cannot do it through the dictation of a bureaucrat. We must do it with your genius, your efforts, your intelligence, and your cooperation.

Now, we have had for a long time a government that applies the philosophy of the left to government. The government will build the power dams, the government will tell you how to distribute your power, the government will do this and that. The government does everything but come in and wash the dishes for the housewife.

Now their answer to evils in government is more government. Take agriculture—they offer us the Brannan Plan. Our health—they offer socialized medicine and want our health to be dictated by some bureaucrat. In the West, they want to make the West a province of government by absentee landlord. If they get away with that, I would like to talk to you people again.

But now, we are never going to surrender these human, these moral obligations that we hold for everyone, the least one of our people. That is America.

No one is going to struggle about that. Every party is going to agree to that. We are going to gain those things by going right down the middle of the road that gives you every opportunity to expand yourself, to earn and save for yourself and your family. We must go forward.

The National Economy (1962)*

John F. Kennedy

... The central domestic problems of our time ... relate not to basic clashes of philosophy or ideology, but to ways and means of reaching common goals—to research for sophisticated solutions to complex and obstinate issues.

---

* From a speech delivered by the President on June 11, 1962, at a Yale University commencement, New Haven, Connecticut.

The world of Calhoun, the world of Taft, had its own hard problems and notable challenges. But its problems are not our problems. Their age is not our age. As every past generation has had to disenthrall itself from an inheritance of truism and stereotypes, so in our time we must move on from the reassuring repetition of stale phrases to a new, difficult but essential confrontation with reality.

For the great enemy of the truth is very often not the lie—deliberate, contrived and dishonest—but the myth—persistent, persuasive and unrealistic.

Too often, we hold fast to cliches of our forbears. We enjoy the comfort of opinion without the discomfort of thought.

Mythology distracts us everywhere—in government as in business, in politics as in economics, in foreign affairs as in domestic affairs.

But today I want to particularly consider the myth and reality in our national economy.

In recent months many have come to feel as I do that the dialogue between the parties—between business and government—between the government and the public—is clogged by illusion and platitude and fails to reflect the true realities of contemporary American society.

.   .   .   .

There are three great ideas of our domestic affairs in which, today, there is a danger that illusion may prevent effective action.

They are:

First, the question of the size and shape of government's responsibilities; second, the question of public fiscal policy; and third, the matter of confidence—business confidence, or public confidence—or simply confidence in America.

I want to talk about all three and I want to talk about them carefully and dispassionately—and I emphasize that I am concerned here not with political debate but with ways to separate false problems from real ones.

If a contest in angry argument were forced upon it, no administration could shrink from response, and history does not suggest that American presidents are totally without resources in an engagement forced upon them because of hostility in one sector of society.

But in the wider national interest we need not partisan wrangling but common concentration on common problems. I came here to this distinguished university to ask you to join in this great task.

Let us take first the question of the size and the shape of government. The myth is that government is big, and bad—and steadily bigger and worse.

Obviously this myth has some excuse for existence. It is true that in recent history each new administration has spent much more money than its predecessors.

Thus President Roosevelt outspent President Hoover and, with allowances for the special case of the Second World War, President Truman outspent President Roosevelt.

Just to prove that this was not a partisan matter, President Eisenhower then outspent President Truman by the handsome figure of $182 billion. It is even possible, some think, that this trend may continue.

But does it follow from this that big government is growing relatively bigger? It does not. For the fact is for the last fifteen years the federal government, and also the federal debt, and also the federal bureaucracy, have grown less rapidly than the economy as a whole.

If we leave defense and space expenditures aside, the federal government since the Second World War has expanded less than any other major section of our national life; less than industry; less than commerce; less than agriculture; less than higher education; and very much less than the noise about big government.

The truth about big government is the truth about any great activity: it is complex. Certainly it is true that size brings dangers, but it is also true that size can bring benefits.

Here at Yale, which has contributed so much to our national progress in science and medicine, it may be proper for me to mention one great and little noticed expansion of government which has brought strength to our whole society: the new role of our federal government as the major patron of research in science and in medicine.

Few people realize that in 1961, in support of all university research in science and medicine, three out of every four dollars came from the federal government. I need hardly point out that this has taken place without undue enlargement of government control; that American scientists remain second to none in their independence and in their individualism.

I am not suggesting that federal expenditure cannot bring on some measure of control. The whole thrust of federal expenditures in agriculture has been related by purpose and design to control, as a means of dealing with the problems created by our farmers and our growing productivity. Each sector, my point is, of activity must be approached on its own merits and in terms of specific national needs.

Generalities in regard to federal expenditures, therefore, can be misleading. Each case—science, urban renewal, agriculture, natural resources—each case must be determined on its merits if we are to profit from our unrivaled ability to combine the strength of public and private purposes.

Next, let us turn to the problem about fiscal myths. Here the myths are legion and the truth hard to find. But let me take as a prime example the problem of the federal budget.

We persist in measuring our federal fiscal integrity today by the conventional, or administrative, budget with results which would be regarded as absurd in any business firm, in any country of Europe, or in any careful assessment of the reality of our national finances.

The administrative budget has sound administrative uses. But for wider purposes it is less helpful. It omits our special trust funds and the effect they have on our economy. It neglects changes in assets or inventories. It cannot tell a loan from a straight expenditure. And worst of all it cannot distinguish between operating expenditures and long-term investments.

This budget in relation to the great problems of federal fiscal policy, which are basic to our country in 1962, is not simply irrelevant; it can be actively misleading. And yet there is a mythology that measures all our national soundness or unsoundness on the single simple basis of this same annual administrative budget.

If our federal budget is to serve not the debate but the country, we must find ways of clarifying this area of discourse.

Still in the area of fiscal policy, let me say a word about deficits. The myth persists that federal deficits create inflation, and budget surpluses prevent it.

Yet sizable budget surpluses after the war did not prevent inflation, and persistent deficits for the last several years have not upset our basic price stability.

Obviously, deficits are sometimes dangerous—and so are surpluses. But honest assessment plainly requires a more sophisticated view than the old and automatic cliche that deficits automatically bring inflation.

There are myths also about our public debt. It is widely supposed that this debt is growing at a dangerously rapid rate. In fact, both the debt per person and the debt as a proportion of our gross national products have declined sharply since the end of the Second World War.

In absolute terms, the national debt since the end of World War II has increased only 8 per cent while private debt was increasing 305 per cent and the debt of state and local governments on whom people frequently suggest we should place additional burden—the debt of state and local government has increased 378 per cent.

Moreover, debts public and private are neither good nor bad in and of themselves. Borrowing can lead to overextension and collapse—but it can also lead to expansion and strength. There is no single simple slogan in this field that we can trust.

Finally, I come to the problem of confidence. Confidence is a matter of myth and also a matter of truth—and this time let me take the truth of the matter first.

It is true and of high importance that the prosperity of this country depends on the assurances that all major elements within it will live up to their responsibilities.

If business were to neglect its obligations to the public; if labor were blind to all public responsibility; above all, if government were to abandon its obvious—and statutory—duty of watchful concern for our economic health—and any of these things should happen—then confidence might well be weakened and the danger of stagnation would increase.

This is the true issue of confidence.

But there is also the false issue—and in its simplest form it is the assertion that any and all unfavorable turns of the speculative wheel—however temporary and however plainly speculative in character—are the result of—and I quote—a lack of confidence in the national administration.

This, I must tell you, while comforting, is not wholly true. Worse, it obscures the reality which is also simple. The solid ground of mutual confidence is the necessary partnership of government with all of the sectors of our society in the steady quest for economic progress.

Corporate plans are not based on a political confidence in party leaders but on an economic confidence in the nation's ability to invest and produce and consume.

Business had full confidence in the administration in power in 1929, 1954, 1958, and 1960. But this was not enough to prevent recession when business lacked full confidence in the economy. What matters is the capacity of the nation as a whole to deal with its economic problems and its opportunities.

The stereotypes I have been discussing distract our attention and divide our efforts. These stereotypes do our nation a disservice not just because they are exhausted and irrelevant, but above all because they are misleading—because they stand in the way of the solution of hard and complicated facts.

It is not new that past debates should obscure present realities. But the damage of such a false dialogue is greater today than ever before simply because today the safety of all the world—the very future of freedom—depends as never before upon the sensible and clearheaded management of the domestic affairs of the United States.

The real issues of our time are rarely as dramatic as the issues of Calhoun's. The differences today are usually matters of degree. And we cannot understand and attack our contemporary problems in 1962 if we are bound by traditional labels and worn-out slogans of an earlier era.

But the unfortunate fact of the matter is that our rhetoric has not kept pace with the speed of social and economic change. Our political debate, our public discourse on current domestic and economic issues, too often bears little or no relation to the actual problems the United States faces.

What is at stake in our economic decisions today is not some grand warfare of rival ideologies which will sweep the country with passion but the practical management of the modern economy. What we need are not labels and cliches but more basic discussion of the sophisticated and technical questions involved in keeping a great economic machinery moving ahead.

The national interest lies in high employment and steady expansion of output and stable prices and a strong dollar. The declaration of such an objective is easy. The attainment in an intricate and interdependent economy and world is a little more difficult. To attain them we require not some automatic response but hard thought.

.   .   .   .

. . . These problems are endlessly complicated. And yet they go to the future of this country and its ability to prove to the world what we believe it must prove. I am suggesting that the problems of fiscal and monetary policy in the sixties as opposed to the kinds of problems we faced in the thirties demand subtle challenges for which technical answers—not political answers—must be provided.

These are matters upon which government and business may, and in many cases will, disagree. They are certainly matters that government and business should be discussing in the most sober, dispassionate and careful way if we are to maintain the kind of vigorous economy upon which our country depends.

How can we develop and sustain strong and stable world markets for basic commodities without unfairness to the consumer and without undue stimulus to the producer?

How can we generate the buying power which can consume what we produce on our farms and in our factories?

How can we take advantage of the miracles of automation with the great demand that it will put upon high-skilled labor and yet offer employment to the half a million of unskilled school dropouts every year who enter the labor market—8 million of them in the 1960's?

How do we eradicate the barriers which separate substantial minorities of our citizens from access to education and employment on equal terms with the rest?

How, in sum, can we make our free economy work at full capacity, that is, provide adequate profits for enterprise and adequate wages for labor and adequate utilization of plant and opportunity for all?

These are the problems that we should be talking about, that the political parties and the various groups in our country should be discussing. They cannot be solved by incantations from the forgotten past.

But the example of Western Europe shows that they are capable of solution. That government, and many of them are conservative governments, prepared to face technical problems without ideological preconceptions, can coordinate the elements of a national economy and bring about growth and prosperity—a decade of them—a decade of them.

Some conversations I have heard in our country sound like old records, long-playing, left over from the middle thirties. The debate of the thirties had its great significance and produced great results. But it took place in a different world with different needs and tasks. It is our responsibility today to live in our own world, and to identify the needs and discharge the tasks of the 1960's.

If there is any current trend toward meeting present problems with old cliches, this is the moment to stop it—before it lands us all in the bog of sterile acrimony.

Discussion is essential, and I am hopeful that the debate of recent weeks, though up to now somewhat barren, may represent the start of a serious dialogue of the kind which has led Europe to such fruitful collaboration among all the elements of economic society and to a decade of unrivaled economic progress.

But let us not engage in the wrong argument at the wrong time, between the wrong people in the wrong country, while the real problems of our time grow and multiply, fertilized by our neglect.

Nearly 150 years ago Thomas Jefferson wrote: "The new circumstances under which we are placed call for new words, new phrases, and the transfer of old words to new objects."

That is truer today than it was in the time of Jefferson, because the role of this country is so vastly more significant.

There is a show in England called "Stop the World, I Want To Get Off." You have not chosen to exercise that option. You are part of the world, and you must participate in these days of our years in the solution of the problems that pour upon us, requiring the most sophisticated and technical judgment.

And, as we work in concert to meet the authentic problems of our time, we will generate a vision and an energy which will demonstrate anew to the world the superior vitality and the strength of the free society.

The Logic of the Welfare State*

Reo M. Christenson

The defenders of the welfare state are convinced, according to Sidney Hook, that the only modern alternative to the welfare state is the "ill-fare" state. They believe the attack is based largely on the ringing affirmation of platitudes that are largely irrelevant to today's society or to the specific problems we face. They are convinced that their opponents take isolated abuses and generalize sweeping indictments from these. And they believe a number of non-sequiturs can be cited that seriously weaken the detractors' case.[1]

Welfare state proponents insist that inadequate recognition is given to the factors producing poverty. These factors, they assert, do not support the rather censorious and patronizing attitude that welfare state critics often seem to hold toward the unfortunate members of society.

The causes of poverty are legion, but these are among the more important: depression or recession, which bring unemployment and economic hardship as a consequence of forces beyond the lone worker's control; automation, which makes working skills obsolete—a particu-

---

* "The Logic of the Welfare State" from *Challenge and Decision: Political Issues of Our Time* by Reo M. Christenson (second edition). Copyright © 1964, 1967 by Reo M. Christenson. Reprinted by permission of Harper & Row, Publishers.

[1] Sidney Hook, "Welfare State—A Debate That Isn't," *The New York Times Magazine* (November 27, 1960).

larly serious disaster to those beyond forty years of age; inflation, which robs savings of their initial purchasing power; accidents or occupational diseases—for which the individual is not personally responsible; other forms of illness, among the paramount causes of poverty; low-grade intelligence, which precludes the individual from earning enough to save for emergencies; emotional instability—the result either of genetic inheritance or of unwholesome family conditions which had a crippling effect on the growing child; loss of the family breadwinner through death, divorce, or desertion; a large family—the care of which leaves no opportunity to accumulate financial reserves; a non-white racial inheritance, which severely limits earning opportunities (one half of Negro families in the South made under $1,200 a year in 1964, and a Negro college graduate typically makes about the same income as a white person with an eighth-grade education); inadequate educational opportunities during one's youth, or the necessity to leave school early to help support the family; and a variety of other factors largely beyond the individual's control. Thus, the implicit (if often unspoken) premise that poverty is largely a moral disease that can be cured if society is "tough enough" with its victims is a premise unsupported by a calm and rational analysis of the facts.

The critics also pass all too lightly over our change from an agrarian society to an urban, industrial society. Farmers can tighten their belts and survive even when economic conditions are desperate; they can take in their parents and in-laws, if necessary, and supply their minimum needs. But urban families cannot be so self-reliant, and their dependence on the proper functioning of the economic system cannot be overestimated. When 12 million persons were unemployed during the Depression, there was no point in exhorting them to be self-reliant and independent and to glory in the disaster that could help them build noble characters. The attempt to transplant the principles and ideals of an agrarian, pioneer society to the industrialized metropolitan complexes of today is as futile and misdirected as an attempt to apply the principles of the guild system to a modern automated factory.

Self-reliance will indeed never become obsolete, but there is ample scope for its operation in the welfare state. The individual who moves beyond the plane of mere survival into the realm of success (however that term is interpreted) will almost always be one who exercises self-reliance, initiative, and personal responsibility in disciplining himself to the effort and sacrifice success entails and in taking advantage of opportunities as they arise.

Everyone agrees that provision of some kind must be made for persons who, for whatever reason, are unable to buy the necessities of life. So the choice is not, "Shall we or shall we not have a welfare state?" but, "What kind of a welfare state shall we have?" Even Elizabethan England had its welfare state—one that established workhouses and imposed the most severe conditions on those unable to care for themselves. The choices, then, are, broadly: a system of private charity or a system of publicly provided assistance drawing on general tax revenues and administered in conjunction with means tests or a system using social insurance to the maximum feasible degree.

The private charity alternative scarcely deserves serious consideration, because it is not only psychologically unsound, but wholly unrealistic. Private charity could never meet the routine demands for help in our great cities, to say nothing of unusual emergencies. It would be spotty, unco-ordinated, uncertain, and chaotic. Although it might be pleasant for the contributors to feel that they had given directly to persons in distress, their satisfaction would be at the expense of the recipients. The latter are often acutely embarrassed at being the object of personal charity. They feel uncomfortably obligated to those who have helped them, and they vastly prefer the impersonality of public relief to the alternative of a psychologically distressing scene in which their helpless and poverty-stricken status is nakedly exposed before their friends and neighbors.

For reasons made clear in an earlier chapter, most welfare state defenders prefer a system relying heavily on social insurance. They believe it (1) relates individual contributions to individual benefits, thereby preventing the growth of a something-for-nothing spirit; (2) avoids the humiliations and degradation accompanying either private charity or means-test public aid; and (3) is more soundly financed.

Does the welfare state actually encourage indolence? The examination of specific programs suggests that this fear is largely groundless. Does workmen's compensation really encourage people to injure themselves so they can collect compensation? Does aid to the blind and crippled and disabled encourage anyone to become blind or crippled or disabled? Does Medicare cause the aged to feign illness? And will the kind of woman who has a succession of illegitimate children while on relief make a rational decision to forgo illicit relations if aid to her children is reduced? Does unemployment compensation encourage idleness (except in rare instances, where cheating admittedly takes place)? If a worker is fired for cause, he does not immediately qualify for benefits. And because unemployment compensation normally returns less than 40 per cent of the worker's wages, how many people—especially men with families—prefer idleness and a 60 per cent income slash to working on a job which provides them not only with some of the comforts everyone wants but also with the self-respect and community respect nearly all men covet? Granted that a few men are indifferent to community disapproval, they usually are such hopeless characters that they will not be shocked into reform by any system of charity.

The social compulsion to work is exceedingly strong in our society. Reinforced by the natural desire for greater material satisfactions and increased security (and further reinforced by the salutary nagging of wives who are outraged if their husbands won't work, and by the readiness of collection agencies to repossess TV sets), these pressures are such that only a tiny percentage of adults will deliberately choose a life of idleness when the alternative is a 150 per cent increase in income. General relief payments, it should be added, are also far below the income workers can obtain through employment.

As for Social Security, it was widely predicted that the guarantee of publicly provided pensions for the aged would seriously discourage private savings and would administer a heavy blow to the private insurance industry. Insurance companies now freely concede that this was a faulty prediction, because insurance has grown at an unprecedented rate since Social Security was introduced. Furthermore, despite the growth of our many-faceted welfare state, there has been no decline in national savings in proportion to national income. This is an extremely important fact, because if the premises of those opposed to the welfare state are correct, a reduction in personal savings should have set in.

During the Depression skeptics insisted that the national relief program had sapped the will to work. When jobs became available during the war, however, virtually every able-bodied person took a job—including more and more women. Experience repeatedly confirms the premise that when jobs are plentiful, unemployed persons as well as many who had not previously listed themselves as unemployed step forward to take those jobs. The criers of alarm have not been vindicated by the objective facts.

But the most compelling evidence that the welfare state does not necessarily impair the willingness to work is provided by the experiences of Western Europe. Sweden, for instance, has long functioned with a generous "cradle-to-grave" welfare state, yet unemployment has been reduced to about 1 per cent in recent years.[2] West Germany has had a highly developed welfare state longer than any other country in the world, yet the West German economy is the most productive in Europe.[3] Other Western European countries also have considerably more advanced welfare states than the United States without suffering any impairment of the willingness to work. During the 1950's, in fact, those countries made considerably more rapid economic advances than the United States, and their percentage of unemployment was generally lower. If the welfare state produced the horrendous results attributed to it, this phenomenon simply would not have occurred.

We are told that under the welfare state much of the challenge of living is removed, and that life takes on a flat and insipid flavor because of the security in which the individual is swaddled. This is an interesting charge, but one that is both superficial and wholly lacking in objective supporting evidence. Does the excitement really go out of life because the bare necessities of life are assured by the state? Does life become dull and tasteless because starvation no longer threatens? Does any reasonable person actually believe that modern life is so bereft of challenge under the welfare state that it no longer calls forth our best? The major challenges of life are still with us: attaining a high degree of competence in a chosen field, as well as broadening and deepening one's range of interests; being the best husband, wife, father, or mother one is capable of becoming; standing up for unpopular causes and beliefs; helping solve any of the manifold knotty community problems that exist; bringing one's intelligence and energies to bear on the great national and international problems. One can even hope to become a millionaire, if that is one's ambition. America has 90,000 of them, and their numbers have been rapidly increasing over the past ten years.

There is no need to deny that a certain amount of hardship and deprivation can have beneficial effects on the formation of character, or that too many comforts and luxuries coming too easily may not only sap the spirit but also reduce a person's capacity to fully enjoy material advantages. But this is largely irrelevant to the question of

[2] For a defense of Sweden's way of life, see Werner Wiskari, "Rejoinder to Sweden's Critics," *The New York Times Magazine* (October 23, 1960), 61. But also see Gunnar Myrdal, "The Swedish Way to Happiness," *The New York Times Magazine* (January 30, 1966). Myrdal takes an ambivalent position.

[3] For a change in German working habits, however, compare Flora Lewis, "Hans Schmidt Lives to Work," *The New York Times Magazine* (May 24, 1959), 15; with "Men of Leisure," *Newsweek* (May 25, 1964), 46, 48.

the welfare state. We are not talking about comforts or luxuries, but only about the subsistence levels provided by social insurance or public assistance. Moreover, do not those who most vociferously proclaim the merits of hardship and adversity do everything in their power to insure that their own children have plenty of nourishing food, warm clothing, adequate shelter, the best educational opportunities, the best medical care, and as many other "advantages" as they can provide? Why is it desirable for some children to enjoy these privileges, but good for other people's children to go without? It must be borne in mind that a large part of the welfare state's benefits go to provide necessities for children. Whatever the shortcomings of their parents, children certainly deserve minimum living standards. These the welfare state is determined to furnish, and this should be a source of national pride rather than a source of reproach.

A growing number of observers think unnecessary poverty, weighing most heavily on children, could be mitigated by a system of family allowances. Canada, for example, pays mothers from six to ten dollars per child per month (up to the age of 16) to help them properly feed, clothe, and care for their offspring. Although the introduction of the program in 1944 was accompanied by predictions of disaster, it has become a highly popular and virtually non-controversial program (as is largely true in the thirty other countries paying family allowances). Nor has it led to an increase in the birth rate, contrary to the prophecies of its critics.

It is argued that the welfare state is all right up to a point, but that we are carrying it too far. This charge, of course, has been made at *each* point along the welfare road. Whenever the state is on the verge of providing a new and needed public service, we are always assured that we are approaching the danger point. The most recent example: for some mystic reason it was desirable to use social insurance to protect the American people against a number of unpredictable financial disasters, but it was thought alarming to use it to protect us against the greatest unpredictable economic disaster—costly illness.

If there is to be protection against illness, why shouldn't the state provide food and clothing and shelter? The answer is simple: it makes sense to protect people against heavy medical bills, but it does not make sense for the government to supply the entire population with the necessities of survival. Unemployment compensation at moderate levels can be intelligently defended, but unemployment compensation which grants the unemployed person almost as much as he would make by working cannot be defended. Aid to the blind can be defended, but not aid to those afflicted with hay fever. A good case can be made for aid to those whose resources are exhausted, but no sensible case can be made for giving these persons income returns approximating those of employed persons. So long as people maintain a modicum of common sense, the state will not undertake absurd social services or absurdly generous benefits.

Those who are most critical of the welfare state basically lack faith in the judgment of a free people to make intelligent decisions. Perhaps their skepticism will some day prove well founded, but there is scanty evidence in the realm of national economic and social legislation to sustain this skepticism. Congressional action in these fields has almost invariably stood the test of time and merited the approbation of subsequent generations. If Congress is to be faulted on this score, its weakness lies in doing too little, too late. Most economists, for instance, believe unemployment compensation should equal 50 to 60 per cent of wages, not 35 to 40 per cent. And most Social Security experts believe Social Security payments have generally erred on the skimpy side. Some people talk as if the life of an ADC mother were a bowl of cherries. Are they aware that the average ADC family of four received the munificent sum of $125 per month in 1965? This is living high on the hog? And do they really believe the ADC mother, before she beds down with some male friend, shrewdly calculates the cash value of the child that may result from the night? In any case, do we want to penalize children for the bad luck of being born to a poor and unfortunate mother?

A more accurate picture of ADC is the following: "The typical ADC mother in Chicago is a poor Negro—the girl left behind to raise illegitimate children. She is insecure, uneducated, unsophisticated, frightened. She lives in a hovel and has no social or recreational outlet. She craves security and is vulnerable to men."[4]

Our choices in dealing with admitted ADC abuses are various: (1) We can, as in Mississippi, make it a crime for a "welfare" mother to give birth to a second illegimate child. But how can an ADC mother pay a fine? And who will care for her children if she goes to jail? (2) We can terminate all aid when an ADC mother has illegitimate children or mis-spends money on alcohol or other non-essentials. But again, should children be punished for parental sins? (3) We can authorize social workers to spend most of the ADC check on essentials, leaving only a few dollars for discretionary spending by the mother.

---

[4] "The Mystery of Rising Relief Costs," *U. S. News and World Report* (March 8, 1965), 41.

This is humiliating, but in extreme cases may well be necessary. (It is a practice already widely followed by welfare departments.) (4) We can raise the minimum wage in order to make employment a more attractive option. (Perhaps this could be done while establishing public day-care nurseries, as in Scandinavia, to better enable mothers to work.) (5) We can devise a system that reduces ADC payments to a working mother but on a scale that maximizes the incentive to work. (6) We can provide an adequate number of psychiatric social workers and other skilled counselors to help the ADC mother with her family and emotional problems. (This is a long-range objective; there is already a grievous shortage of such personnel.)

Some of these choices have much to commend them. If the critics of the welfare state wish to concentrate on constructive recommendations, friends of the welfare state welcome their contributions.

Log-rolling is indubitably a characteristic of the American legislative way, and it is an untidy, undisciplined, and sometimes wasteful way to conduct the public business. But it is the American way of forming legislative majorities in the absence of cohesive, disciplined political parties. Those who solemnly warn of its costs generally do so only when Congress is considering measures they dislike, not when Congress acts in areas in which they feel action is needed. The prospect of log-rolling cannot be logically used as an excuse for legislative inaction where urgent problems exist, or legislative paralysis would set in. The same applies to the argument concerning the future of agencies that have outlived their usefulness. Of course new programs should not be established until mature deliberation has demonstrated their need, but the prolonged nature of our legislative process normally insures that this takes place. Does any knowledgeable person really believe it is easy to persuade Congress to innovate—especially where money is involved?

Where will the welfare state end? No one can answer with certainty, but the experience of Western Europe provides a solid basis for optimism in the ultimate judgment of a free people. Most Western European nations have rounded out their welfare states with national health insurance—and then turned their attention primarily to increasing productivity. Although children's allowances are provided in some of these states and sickness compensation (in addition to medical insurance) in others, the political parties generally have not sought the continuous extension of the welfare state in pursuit of votes. It is not too difficult to convince the people that welfare programs must be paid for, and therefore they should be instituted only when a rational case can be made on their behalf. The onward march of the welfare state has been substantially halted in Europe because state services in this area have substantially fulfilled their potentially useful role. We can assume that American public opinion will be no less enlightened than its European counterpart.

Isn't the comparison with ancient Rome rather strained? The Roman Empire was supporting a swarm of permanently idle persons without making any real attempt to find work for them. No re-employment training programs were in effect, nor were there tools at hand to stimulate their economy into full production. It was not a disgrace to be idle, nor did the shops bulge with the kind of goods that make materialists out of all but the hardiest modern consumers. Rome supported its idle with grain wrested from conquered territories, whereas America engages in major foreign aid programs to help other countries. The widespread ownership of property, the work ethic, the humbler role of the military, the successful operation of a democratic system, the relative absence of graft in our national public service— in these and a hundred other characteristics America differs from those evils of ancient Rome that ultimately brought about its downfall. America may or may not be in a period of moral decline, but what reputable sociologist attributes our moral problems to the existence of the welfare state?

The welfare state is indeed costly, but if the money is well spent for necessary purposes, it is a justified cost. It is one mark of an enlightened state that it makes adequate provision to meet the needs of its people; savings achieved at the expense of human misery are indefensible. The blind, the crippled, the needy children, the jobless, the aged without necessary resources, and so on—these unfortunates surely deserve help from a society as affluent as ours. . . .

Chapter Four

The War On Poverty

By the middle sixties it became increasingly clear that no single problem so tested the welfare state's ability to cope with contemporary realities as did the matter of urban poverty. One passionate writer after another poured forth disillusionment and disgust with a society steeped in material achievement and yet afflicted with millions of poor. One set after another of cold statistics buttressed these contentions, and the attentions of the administrations of Presidents Kennedy and Johnson turned towards attempts at solution. For it had become not merely a source of embarrassment to America, not only a bothersome afterthought, but truly a testing of our oft-declared ideals and commitments toward the building of the Great Society.

In the section that follows we present, therefore, the program of a president, the data of an economist, and the indictment and pleading of a concerned humanist.

Message on Poverty (1964)*

Lyndon B. Johnson

We are citizens of the richest and most fortunate nation in the history of the world.

---

* From Message to the Congress of the United States on the Economic Opportunity Act of 1964 by President Lyndon B. Johnson, March 16, 1964.

One hundred and eighty years ago we were a small country struggling for survival on the margin of a hostile land.

Today we have established a civilization of free men which spans an entire continent.

With the growth of our country has come opportunity for our people—opportunity to educate our children, to use our energies in productive work, to increase our leisure—opportunity for almost every American to hope that through work and talent he could create a better life for himself and his family.

The path forward has not been an easy one.

But we have never lost sight of our goal—an America in which every citizen shares all the opportunities of his society, in which every man has a chance to advance his welfare to the limit of his capacities.

We have come a long way toward this goal.

We still have a long way to go.

The distance which remains is the measure of the great unfinished work of our society.

To finish that work I have called for a national war on poverty. Our objective—total victory.

There are millions of Americans—one-fifth of our people—who have not shared in the abundance which has been granted to most of us, and on whom the gates of opportunity have been closed.

What does this poverty mean to those who endure it?

It means a daily struggle to secure the necessities for even a meager existence. It means that the abundance, the comforts, the opportunities they see all around them are beyond their grasp.

Worst of all, it means hopelessness for the young.

The young man or woman who grows up without a decent education, in a broken home, in a hostile and squalid environment, in ill health or in the face of racial injustice—that young man or woman is often trapped in a life of poverty.

He does not have the skills demanded by a complex society. He does not know how to acquire those skills. He faces a mounting sense of despair which drains initiative and ambition and energy.

Our tax cut will create millions of new jobs—new exits from poverty.

But we must also strike down all the barriers which keep many from using those exits.

The war on poverty is not a struggle simply to support people, to make them dependent on the generosity of others.

It is a struggle to give people a chance.

It is an effort to allow them to develop and use their capacities, as we have been allowed to develop and use ours, so that they can share, as others share, in the promise of this nation.

We do this, first of all, because it is right that we should.

From the establishment of public education and land-grant colleges through agricultural extension and encouragement to industry we have pursued the goal of a nation with full and increasing opportunities for all its citizens. The war on poverty is a further step in that pursuit.

We do it also because helping some will increase the prosperity of all.

Our fight against poverty will be an investment in the most valuable of our resources—the skills and strength of our people.

And in the future, as in the past, this investment will return its cost manyfold to our entire economy.

If we can raise the annual earnings of 10 million among the poor by only $1,000 we will have added $14 billion a year to our national output. In addition we can make important reductions in public assistance payments which now cost us $4 billion a year, and in the large costs of fighting crime and delinquency, disease and hunger.

This is only part of the story.

Our history has proved that each time we broaden the base of abundance, giving more people the chance to produce and consume, we create new industry, higher production, increased earnings, and better income for all.

Giving new opportunity to those who have little will enrich the lives of all the rest.

Because it is right, because it is wise, and because, for the first time in our history, it is possible to conquer poverty, I submit, for the consideration of the Congress and the country, the Economic Opportunity Act of 1964.

This act does not merely expand old programs or improve what is already being done. It charts a new course. It strikes at the causes, not just the consequences of poverty. It can be a milestone in our 180-year search for a better life for our people.

This act provides five basic opportunities:

It will give almost half a million underprivileged young Americans the opportunity to develop skills, continue education, and find useful work.

It will give every American community the opportunity to develop a comprehensive plan to fight its own poverty—and help them to carry out their plans.

It will give dedicated Americans the opportunity to enlist as volunteers in the war against poverty.

It will give many workers and farmers the opportunity to break through particular barriers which bar their escape from poverty.

It will give the entire nation the opportunity for a concerted attack on poverty through the establishment, under my direction, of the Office of Economic Opportunity, a national headquarters for the war against poverty.

This is how we propose to create these opportunities.

First, we will give high priority to helping young Americans who lack skills, who have not completed their education or who cannot complete it because they are too poor.

The years of high school and college age are the most critical stage of a young person's life. If they are not helped then, many will be condemned to a life of poverty which they, in turn, will pass on to their children.

I, therefore, recommend the creation of a Job Corps, a work-training program, and a work-study program.

A new national Job Corps will build toward an enlistment of 100,000 young men. They will be drawn from those whose background, health, and education make them least fit for useful work.

Those who volunteer will enter more than 100 camps and centers around the country.

Half of these young men will work, in the first year, on special conservation projects to give them education, useful work experience and to enrich the natural resources of the country.

Half of these young men will receive, in the first year, a blend of training, basic education and work experience in job training centers.

These are not simply camps for the underprivileged. They are new educational institutions, comparable in innovation to the land-grant colleges. Those who enter them will emerge better qualified to play a productive role in American society.

A new national work-training program operated by the Department of Labor will provide work and training for 200,000 American men and women between the ages of 16 and 21. This will be developed through state and local governments and non-profit agencies.

Hundreds of thousands of young Americans badly need the experience, the income, and the sense of purpose which useful full- or part-time work can bring. For them such work may mean the difference between finishing school or dropping out. Vital community activities from hospitals and playgrounds to libraries and settlement houses are suffering because there are not enough people to staff them.

We are simply bringing these needs together.

A new national work-study program operated by the Department of Health, Education, and Welfare will provide federal funds for part-time jobs for 140,000 young Americans who do not go to college because they cannot afford it.

There is no more senseless waste than the waste of the brainpower and skill of those who are kept from college by economic circumstance. Under this program they will, in a great American tradition, be able to work their way through school.

They and the country will be richer for it.

Second, through a new community action program we intend to strike at poverty at its source—in the streets of our cities and on the farms of our countryside among the very young and the impoverished old.

This program asks men and women throughout the country to prepare long-range plans for the attack on poverty in their own local communities.

These are not plans prepared in Washington and imposed upon hundreds of different situations.

They are based on the fact that local citizens best understand their own problems, and know best how to deal with those problems.

These plans will be local plans striking at the many unfilled needs which underlie poverty in each community, not just one or two. Their components and emphasis will differ as needs differ.

These plans will be local plans calling upon all the resources available to the community—federal and state, local and private, human and material.

And when these plans are approved by the Office of Economic Opportunity, the federal government will finance up to 90 per cent of the additional cost for the first two years.

The most enduring strength of our nation is the huge reservoir of talent, initiative, and leadership which exists at every level of our society.

Through the community action program we call upon this, our greatest strength, to overcome our greatest weakness.

Third, I ask for the authority to recruit and train skilled volunteers for the war against poverty.

Thousands of Americans have volunteered to serve the needs of other lands.

Thousands more want the chance to serve the needs of their own land.

They should have that chance.

Among older people who have retired, as well as among the young, among women as well as men, there are many Americans who are ready to enlist in our war against poverty.

They have skills and dedication. They are badly needed.

If the state requests them, if the community needs and will use them, we will recruit and train them and give them the chance to serve.

Fourth, we intend to create new opportunities for certain hard-hit groups to break out of the pattern of poverty.

Through a new program of loans and guarantees we can provide incentives to those who will employ the unemployed.

Through programs of work and retraining for unemployed fathers and mothers we can help them support their families in dignity while preparing themselves for new work.

Through funds to purchase needed land, organize co-operatives, and create new and adequate family farms we can help those whose life on the land has been a struggle without hope.

Fifth, I do not intend that the war against poverty becomes a series of unco-ordinated and unrelated efforts—that it perish for lack of leadership and direction.

Therefore this bill creates, in the Executive Office of the President, a new Office of Economic Opportunity. Its Director will be my personal chief of staff for the war against poverty. I intend to appoint Sargent Shriver to this post.

He will be directly responsible for these new programs. He will work with and through existing agencies of the government.

This program—the Economic Opportunity Act—is the foundation of our war against poverty. But it does not stand alone.

For the past three years this government has advanced a number of new proposals which strike at important areas of need and distress.

I ask the Congress to extend those which are already in action, and to establish those which have already been proposed.

There are programs to help badly distressed areas such as the Area Redevelopment Act, and the legislation now being prepared to help Appalachia.

There are programs to help those without training find a place in today's complex society—such as the Manpower Development Training Act and the Vocational Education Act for youth.

There are programs to protect those who are specially vulnerable to the ravages of poverty—hospital insurance for the elderly, protection for migrant farmworkers, a food stamp program for the needy, coverage for millions not now protected by a minimum wage, new and expanded unemployment benefits for men out of work, a housing and community development bill for those seeking decent homes.

Finally there are programs which help the entire country, such as aid to education which, by raising the quality of schooling available to every American child, will give a new chance for knowledge to the children of the poor.

I ask immediate action on all these programs.

What you are being asked to consider is not a simple or an easy program. But poverty is not a simple or an easy enemy.

It cannot be driven from the land by a single attack on a single front. Were this so, we would have conquered poverty long ago.

Nor can it be conquered by government alone.

For decades American labor and American business, private institutions and private individuals have been engaged in strengthening our economy and offering new opportunity to those in need.

We need their help, their support, and their full participation.

Through this program we offer new incentives and new opportunities for co-operation, so that all the energy of our nation, not merely the efforts of government, can be brought to bear on our common enemy.

Today, for the first time in our history, we have the power to strike away the barriers to full participation in our society. Having the power, we have the duty.

The Congress is charged by the Constitution to "provide . . . for the general welfare of the United States." Our present abundance is a measure of its success in fulfilling that duty. Now Congress is being asked to extend that welfare to all our people.

The president of the United States is president of all the people in every section of the country. But this office also holds a special responsibility to the distressed and disinherited, the hungry and the hopeless of this abundant nation.

It is in pursuit of that special responsibility that I submit this message to you today.

The new program I propose is within our means. Its cost of $970 million is 1 per cent of our national budget—and every dollar I am requesting for this program is already included in the budget I sent to Congress in January.

But we cannot measure its importance by its cost.

For it charts an entirely new course of hope for our people.

We are fully aware that this program will not eliminate all the poverty in America in a few months or a few years. Poverty is deeply rooted and its causes are many.

But this program will show the way to new opportunities for millions of our fellow citizens.

It will provide a lever with which we can begin to open the door to our prosperity for those who have been kept outside.

It will also give us the chance to test our weapons, to try our energy and ideas and imagination for the many battles yet to come. As conditions change, and as experience illuminates our difficulties, we will be prepared to modify our strategy.

And this program is much more than a beginning.

Rather it is a commitment. It is a total commitment by this President, and this Congress, and this nation, to pursue victory over the most ancient of mankind's enemies.

On many historic occasions the president has requested from Congress the authority to move against forces which were endangering the well-being of our country.

This is such an occasion.

On similar occasions in the past we have often been called upon to wage war against foreign enemies which threatened our freedom. Today we are asked to declare war on a domestic enemy which threatens the strength of our nation and the welfare of our people.

If we now move forward against this enemy—if we can bring to the challenges of peace the same determination and strength which has brought us victory in war—then this day and this Congress will have won a secure and honorable place in the history of the nation, and the enduring gratitude of generations of Americans yet to come.

The Composition of the Poor*

Herman P. Miller

The inclusion of a paper on counting up the poor in a session devoted to income redistribution policies can only mean that we wish to take a backward glance at the dimensions of poverty as we move forward in the search for new solutions to this ancient problem. It is fortunate that our policies in this and other areas do not await the perfection of statistics. If they did, we might find ourselves suffering intolerable evils for want of a proper measure. At the same time we must recognize that blind action, unaccompanied by a solid factual base, can be equally dangerous. It is important, therefore, that, as we forge new programs designed to alleviate poverty, we re-examine our concepts and our statistical measures to make certain that we can properly appraise the results of our efforts.

In this paper I do not intend to focus on the shortcomings of statistics on the distribution of income, because they are widely known. Many authors have written about the problems associated with the inaccuracies in the data, the use of a money income concept, the use of a single year's income, the changes in family composition, the failure to account properly for the increased tendency of the young and the old to live alone, etc. I do feel compelled to say, however, that, although the status of our knowledge in this area is better than it was thirty years ago when we first started collecting income data systematically, it is still deplorable. Only six months ago T. W. Schultz wrote, "Our President is now focusing attention on poverty in the United States. But unfortunately we are ill prepared to act because we have been out of touch. . . . All we have is a handful of crude data, mostly on family incomes, and they tell us very little."[1] Similar statements were made years ago by Dorothy Brady, Simon Kuznets, and other leaders in the field.

Although the problems have been known for a long time, the solutions have not been forthcoming. The Census Bureau, for example, is still compiling income statistics according to the same procedures and definitions that were used twenty years ago when the annual

---

1 Theodore W. Schultz, "Our Welfare State and the Welfare of Farm People," *Social Service Review*, XXXVIII (June, 1964), 123–129.

income survey was introduced as an experimental innovation. After nearly a quarter of a century of experience, it is time to move on to more sophisticated statistical approaches to the problem and to new data that are more specifically oriented to the problem as it is viewed today.

Revised Estimates of Poverty

Figures recently published by the federal government provide the best measure of the number and characteristics of the poor that has been available since the onset of the current debate on poverty. When the Council of Economic Advisers made its study of poverty several years ago, it used a cash income of less than $3,000 in 1962 as the poverty line for families of two or more persons and income of less than $1,500 for unrelated individuals (persons living alone or with non-relatives). The failure to take various factors like size of family, the age of family head, and farm residence into account was recognized as a serious shortcoming that had to be tolerated because of the lack of more refined estimates. Early this year, however, the Department of Health, Education, and Welfare retabulated the Census Bureau's sample statistics for 1963, using a flexible poverty line which eliminates many of the shortcomings cited above.

The basic procedure employed in preparing the revised estimates involves the use of an economy budget, developed by the Department of Agriculture, which specifies in great detail the weekly quantities of foods needed by men, women, and children in various age groups in order to maintain nutritional adequacy. According to the HEW report, this budget, which is "adapted to the food patterns of families in the lowest third of the income range, has for many years been used by welfare agencies as a basis for food allotments for needy families."[2] Using the quantities specified in the budget and food prices published by the Department of Agriculture, annual estimates of food costs needed to maintain nutritional adequacy were prepared for 124 different types of families classified by farm and non-farm residence, age and sex of head, and number of children. These annual food costs were converted to incomes on the basis of assumed relationships between food expenditures and total income.

Families of three or more persons were assumed to be in poverty if their income was less than 33 per cent of the cost of the economy food budget. The poverty line for these families was obtained by

---

[2] Mollie Orshansky, "Counting the Poor: Another Look at the Poverty Profile," *Social Security Bulletin*, XXVIII (January, 1965), 3–29.

multiplying the cost of the food budget by a factor of three. Data recently available from the 1960 Survey of Consumer Expenditures suggest that this is a reasonable relationship between income and food expenditures for low-income families.[3] A ratio of 27 per cent was used for two-person families, while unrelated individuals were assumed to need 80 per cent of the requirement for a couple, "on the premise that the lower the income the more difficult it would be for one person to cut expenses such as housing and utilities below the minimum for a couple."[4] The estimates for farm families are based on the assumption that they would need 40 per cent less cash income than non-farm families of the same size and type, since many farmers receive part of their food and most of their housing without cash payment.

A summary of the dollar values used as the poverty line for selected types of families is shown in Table 1. The poverty line of $3,130 for a non-farm family of four assumes that a daily expenditure of 70 cents per person will provide an adequate diet and that an additional $1.40

Table 1. *Selected Poverty Income Criteria for Families, by Size, Sex of Head, and Residence, United States, 1963*

Number of persons in family	Income on non-farm residence		Income on farm residence	
	Male head	Female head	Male head	Female head
1 (under age 65)	$1,650	$1,525	$ 990	$ 920
1 (aged 65 or over)	1,480	1,465	890	880
2 (under age 65)	2,065	1,875	1,240	1,180
2 (aged 65 and over)	1,855	1,845	1,110	1,120
3	2,455	2,350	1,410	1,395
4	3,130	3,115	1,925	1,865
5	3,685	3,660	2,210	2,220
6	4,135	4,110	2,495	2,530
7 or more	5,100	5,000	3,065	2,985

Source: Mollie Orshansky, "Counting the Poor: Another Look at the Poverty Profile," *Social Security Bulletin*, XXVIII (January, 1965), Table E.

per person will provide for all other needs—housing, clothing, medical care, transportation, etc. The poverty lines for other family types are designed to provide equivalent levels of living. Using these dollar values,

---

[3] Helen H. Lamale, "Expenditure Patterns of Low Consumption Families," paper presented at the December, 1964 meeting of the American Statistical Association.

[4] Orshansky, *op. cit.*

retabulation were made of the income data from the March 1964 Current Population Survey, comparing the income reported for each family with the income "required" by that family. If the reported income was below the required amount for that family type, the family was classified as poor. Families identified as poor on this basis were then retabulated according to various characteristics.

An examination of the revised estimates of poverty shows that, in 1963, about 34.5 million persons were in families with incomes insufficient to purchase an adequate budget. They constituted slightly less than one-fifth (18 per cent) of all persons in the United States. About 5 million lived alone or with non-relatives and 30 million were members of family groups. One-half of the 30 million were children, the great majority of whom were living with both parents (Table 2).

A comparison of the economy budget estimates with those that would have been obtained by the application of the cruder standards used by the Council of Economic Advisers shows a remarkable similarity in the overall totals. The CEA standards would have produced

Table 2. Persons in Poverty Status in 1963, by Alternative Definitions (Number in Millions)

Type of unit	Total U. S. population	Below the economy budget[a]		Below the CEA definition[b]	
		Number	Per cent of total	Number	Per cent of total
All persons	187.2	34.6	18	33.4	18
Farm	12.6	3.2	25	4.9	39
Non-farm	174.6	31.4	18	28.5	16
Unrelated individuals	11.2	4.9	44	4.9	44
Members of families	176.0	29.7	17	28.5	16
Children under 18	68.8	15.0	22	10.8	16

[a] Economy level of the poverty index developed by the Social Security Administration by family size and farm–non-farm residence, centering around $3,100 for four persons.

[b] Interim measure used by Council of Economic Advisors—under $3,000 for families and under $1,500 for unrelated individuals.

Source: Mollie Orshansky, "Counting the Poor: Another Look at the Poverty Profile," Social Security Bulletin, XXVIII (January, 1965), Table 1.

about 33.5 million persons in poverty, or approximately one million less than the number based on the economy budget. The CEA standard would also have produced an additional 1.5 million impoverished farm residents (because of the failure to take non-cash income into account), and, most significantly, 4 million fewer impoverished children (because no adjustment was made for size of family).

Leading characteristics of families with incomes below the economy budget are shown in Table 3. Attention is called here to some of the more significant highlights:

Table 3. Selected Characteristics of Families in Poverty Status in 1963, by Alternative Definitions (Number in Millions)

Selected characteristics	Total number of families	Families below economy budget		Families with incomes under $3,000	
		Number	Per cent of total	Number	Per cent of total
All families	47.4	7.2	15	8.8	19
Residence					
Farm	3.1	0.7	23	1.3	43
Non-farm	44.3	6.5	15	7.5	17
Color					
White	42.7	5.2	12	6.8	16
Non-white	4.7	2.0	42	2.0	43
Age of Head					
14 to 24 years	2.7	0.7	26	0.8	30
25 to 64 years	38.0	5.0	13	4.9	13
65 years and over	6.7	1.5	24	3.1	45
Type of Family					
Male head	42.5	5.2	12	6.5	15
Female head	4.9	2.0	40	2.3	47
Size of Family					
2 persons	15.3	2.5	16	4.6	30
3–5 persons	25.5	2.9	11	3.2	13
6 or more persons	6.6	1.8	27	1.0	15
Employment Status of Head					
Not in labor force	8.8	3.0	34	4.3	49
Unemployed	1.4	0.4	28	0.4	28
Employed	37.2	3.7	10	4.1	11
Work Experience of Head in 1963					
Worked in 1963	40.7	4.6	11	5.1	13
Worked at full-time jobs	37.9	3.6	10	3.8	10
50–52 weeks	30.7	2.0	7	2.1	7
Worked at part-time jobs	2.8	1.0	36	1.4	50
Did not work	6.7	2.6	38	3.7	55

Source: Mollie Orshansky, "Counting the Poor: Another Look at the Poverty Profile," Social Security Bulletin, XXVIII (January, 1965), Table 2.

(a) About 7 million families and 5 million unrelated individuals were in poverty in 1963. Their aggregate income was $11.5 billion below their estimated minimum requirements. This amount might be regarded as a rough estimate of the cost of raising the incomes of all families and individuals above the poverty line as that term is now defined.

(b) Although the 2 million families with a female head accounted for about one-fourth of the poor families, they accounted for nearly one-half of the income gap between actual receipts and minimum requirements. At a cost of about $5 billion all families with a female head could be provided with incomes sufficient to meet minimum requirements as that term is currently defined.

(c) About 2 million families (about a fourth of all the poor families) were headed by a person who worked full-time throughout the year. Increases in aggregate demand and a full-employment economy probably would not benefit these families, except perhaps by providing work for wives and children.[5] Although the heads of this large segment of poor families were fully employed, their incomes were insufficient to raise their families above the poverty line. As an incidental fact, it may be noted that, if the families with a female or a non-white head are subtracted from the total, we find 1.3 million poor families (about 20 per cent of the total) headed by a white man who was fully employed throughout the year. These figures dramatize the fact that low wages are still a major cause of poverty in the United States.

(d) About 1.5 million family heads worked at full-time jobs, but did not work throughout the year. The poverty of these families was attributable to a combination of low wage rates and periods of idleness associated largely with unemployment or illness. Although today's poor are frequently presented as psychologically or spiritually handicapped, the fact is that about 50 per cent of them are headed by a full-time worker whose wages are simply too low to support a family.

(e) The 2 million non-white families constituted about one-fourth of the poor families. About 40 per cent of these families were headed by women, few of whom had year-round full-time employment. A very large proportion of non-white poor live in the South; only about one-fourth live in large metropolitan areas in the North or West.

---

[5] If aggregate demand were increased to the point at which there was an extreme shortage of unskilled labor, there might be a tendency for the wages of the unskilled to rise more rapidly than the wages of skilled workers, as was the case during World War II. Such a situation is highly unlikely today, and, even if it existed, it would be accompanied by severe inflationary pressures.

(f) The 1.5 million families with an aged head constitute about one-fifth of the poor families. The aged are a far smaller fraction of the poor when the economy budget rather than a flat $3,000 is used as the poverty line.

Is Poverty Being Reduced Fast Enough?

The chapter on poverty in the *Economic Report of the President* for 1964 begins with a call to action. It states that we have "been erasing mass poverty in America. But the process is far too slow. It is high time to redouble and to concentrate our efforts to eliminate poverty."[6] The reason for haste, presumably, is that poverty, in the eyes of the Council of Economic Advisers, has become an anachronism in our society. We tolerated it in an earlier era because we had no choice. Now, however, we have it within our means to raise the floor below which we will not let people fall. Since poverty can now be eliminated, the report argues, it should be.

There is an implication in the Economic Report that there has been a slowdown in recent years in the rate at which poverty is being reduced. The report states that "from 1957 through 1962, when total growth was slower and unemployment substantially higher (than in 1947–1956), the number of families in poverty fell less rapidly."[7] The statement is carefully phrased in terms of the *number* rather than the *proportion* of families below the poverty line. The latter, however, is the more critical relationship since the number of families is constantly rising over time.

An examination of the basic figures used by the CEA shows that between 1947 and 1963 the proportion of families with incomes below $3,000 (in terms of 1962 purchasing power) dropped from 32 per cent to 19 per cent (Table 4). In other words, during this sixteen-year period we moved 40 per cent of the way toward the complete eradication of poverty as that term is now defined. Between 1947 and 1956 the proportion of families with incomes under $3,000 dropped from 32 per cent to 23 per cent or at the rate of one percentage point per year. There was no change between 1956 and 1958. Since that time the proportion of families below the $3,000 poverty line dropped once again from 23 per cent to 19 per cent or just under one percentage point per year.

---

6 *Economic Report of the President* (January, 1964), p. 55.

7 *Ibid.*, p. 60.

*Table 4. Per Cent of Families with Money Income Less than $3,000,
1947–1963 (1962 Dollars)*

Year	Per cent of families
1947	32
1950	32
1951	29
1952	28
1953	26
1954	28
1955	25
1956	23
1957	23
1958	23
1959	22
1960	21
1961	21
1962	20
1963	19

Source: Figures for 1947 to 1962 from *Economic Report of the President*, 1964, p. 57; estimate for 1963 derived from U. S. Bureau of the Census, *Current Population Reports—Consumer Income*, Series P–60, No. 43.

In other words, the experience in the reduction of poverty from 1958 to 1963 was not appreciably different from the experience during the decade immediately following the Second World War. Even if the reduction in the incidence of poverty during recent years had been less rapid, the slower progress would not necessarily have been attributable to a slowdown in the rate of economic growth as alleged by the Council. In the first place, as the numerical base diminished it becomes increasingly difficult to achieve the same absolute rate of reduction in the incidence of poverty. It was much easier to reduce the incidence of poverty by one percentage point when one-third of the families were below the poverty line than it is at present when fewer than one-fifth are at that level. Moreover, we must remember that, as we get closer to the very bottom of the income distribution, we are dealing increasingly with the hard-core poor whose incomes in a large proportion of the cases arise outside of the labor market and are not necessarily responsive to economic growth.

Although economic growth tends to reduce poverty by pushing families above the poverty line, it also tends to increase poverty in a statistical sense by making it possible for the young and the old to maintain their own residences, thereby creating large numbers of low-income families that might not otherwise exist as independent units. The available statistics suggest that the observed reductions in poverty during the 1950's were not appreciably affected by these kinds of statistical aberrations. If we examine, for example, changes in the incidence among urban families headed by a person 35 to 44 years of age (Table 5), we find trends that closely parallel those noted

Table 5. Per Cent of Urban Families with Head 35–44 Years of Age with Incomes under $3,000, 1947–1960 (1959 Dollars)

Year	Per cent of urban families
1947	20
1948	20
1949	21
1951	17
1952	16
1953	15
1954	14
1955	11
1956	10
1957	12
1958	11
1959	11
1960	11

Source: Data for 1947–1960 from Herman P. Miller, *Trends in the Income of Families and Persons in the United States: 1947 to 1960*, U. S. Bureau of the Census, Technical Paper No. 8, Table 3.

for the entire population. Since this group of families is not likely to be affected by the process of fractionalization described above, it can be inferred that the change in the incidence of poverty among them reflects the impact of economic forces.

In general, it appears that the conclusions based on data for all families do not require significant alteration when changes in the living arrangements and in the urban–rural distribution of the population are taken into account. A more sensitive test of this thesis can be made by the application of a standardization procedure to the data. The actual percentage distributions for families by residence and age of head are available for each year since 1947. If a constant set of population weights is applied to these data, estimates can be made of the change in the proportion of families below the poverty line, independent of changes in the residence or age distribution of the population. The application of this standardization procedure to the data produced results that did not differ appreciably from the unadjusted data shown in Table 4.

Is the Composition of the Poor Changing?

This is an important question, and it is one that we should be able to answer on the basis of available data; yet it turns out to be quite complex. If $3,000 (in terms of 1962 purchasing power) is used as the poverty line, we can agree unequivocally with the Council of Economic Advisers that "certain handicapping characteristics, notably old age, or absence of an earner or of a male head, have become increasingly prominent in the poor population."[8] We find that in 1963, 35 per cent of the families with incomes under $3,000 were aged as compared with only 26 per cent in 1951 (Table 6). Similarly the proportion of broken families among the poor increased from 19 per cent to 26 per

Table 6. Selected Characteristics of "Poor" Families, 1951 and 1963

Family income for selected year	Per cent of families with family head characteristics		
	65 years and over	Female	Non-white
1951			
Under $2,000 (current dollars)	32	23	21
Under $3,000 (1962 dollars)	26	19	20
1963			
Under $3,000 (1962 dollars)	35	26	23

Source: Derived from U. S. Bureau of the Census, *Current Population Reports —Consumer Income*, Series P–60, Nos. 12 and 43.

cent, and the proportion of non-white families increased from 20 per cent to 23 per cent. All of these changes support the conclusion of the Council.

However, is $3,000 the appropriate poverty line for 1951? The congressional study of low-income families that was conducted in 1949 used $2,000 as the poverty line for that year. Evidently the contemporary conception of poverty that prevailed in the United States shortly after the Second World War called for a poverty line of about $2,000. Are we justified in changing our conception of poverty for this

---

[8] *Ibid.*, p. 72.

earlier period and imposing a new and higher poverty line merely because our current standards have changed? I think not. If we examine the composition of the poor using a $2,000 poverty line for 1951 (in current dollars) and a $3,000 poverty line for 1963 (also in current dollars) we find very much smaller changes in the composition of the poor than those cited above. The aged, for example, represented 32 per cent of the poor in 1951, using the $2,000 poverty line for that year, and 35 per cent of the poor in 1963, using the $3,000 poverty line. Similarly, broken families constituted 23 per cent of the poor in 1951 and 26 per cent in 1963.

Thus, the use of contemporary definitions of poverty suggests that there has been very little change in the composition of the poor, whereas the use of a fixed poverty line suggests that there has been a great deal of change. The reason for the difference is obvious when the underlying statistics are considered. The magnitude of poverty and the characteristics of the poor depend to a large extent on the location of the poverty line. The aged, broken families, and similar disadvantaged groups will be prominent among the poor if a low poverty line is used. As the poverty line is moved closer to the middle of the distribution there is a greater tendency to include average families rather than those with special characteristics. In 1951, an income of $3,000 (in 1962 purchasing power) represented the lowest third of the income distribution, whereas in 1963 the same income represented the lowest fifth. Since the $3,000 poverty line in 1951 was much closer to the middle of the distribution, the aged and broken families represented far smaller fractions of the poor.

The question of the appropriate poverty line that should be used for historical analysis is only now receiving mature consideration. The historical analysis of the change in the number and composition of the poor in the *Economic Report of the President* for 1964 is in terms of a fixed poverty line of $3,000. All references in that report to the elimination of poverty must be construed as the elevation of families above the $3,000 mark measured in terms of 1962 purchasing power.

This static view of the poverty line was more specifically stated in a recent article by Robert Lampman in which he said, "the precise income level selected to mark off poverty from non-poverty is not critical, *so long as it is unchanged over time*, except for necessary adjustments relative to the prevailing price level."[9] This position may represent sound strategy for a short-term viewpoint; however, it is fraught

---

[9] Robert J. Lampman, "One-fifth of a Nation," *Challenge* (April, 1964), 12.

with peril for historical analysis. Moreover, it represents economically unsound thinking for a dynamic society and is at variance with the way in which we have actually gone about measuring poverty at different points in time.

The essential weakness of this position can perhaps best be seen by re-examining some of the observations made about the poverty line in 1904 by Robert Hunter who made one of the first quantitative studies of poverty in the United States. In this study, which is most sympathetic to the plight of the poor, Hunter states, "However desirable and socially valuable an income of $754 a year for each family would be, it is unquestionably too high for a fair estimate of the minimum necessary one. . . . To estimate in the most conservative way possible, let us take more or less arbitrarily $460 a year as essential to defray the expenses of an average family—a father, a mother, and three children—in the cities and industrial communities. . . . In the South, about $300 a year would probably cover the cost of like necessities."[10] Even if we allow for a tripling of prices since 1900, it is apparent that at the turn of the century Hunter could not conceive of a poverty line as high as $2,000 (in current dollars) for a family of five living in a metropolitan area.

We can see what a disservice Hunter would have done to the cause of the poor if he had been willing to settle for a fixed poverty line based on the experience of his time.

There is ample evidence of a relatively sharp upward movement in the poverty line even during the short period since the end of World War II. As previously noted, when the Joint Economic Committee made the first congressional investigation of low-income families in 1949 the poverty line was set at $2,000 for a family of two or more persons. Price increases since that time should have raised the level to about $2,500 in 1962; but the poverty line actually used in 1962 was $3,000, an increase of about 20 per cent in thirteen years, or roughly 1.5 per cent per year. Further evidence of this tendency is provided by BLS data which show that the cost of a "modest but adequate" level of living (excluding taxes) for a working-class family of four persons in New York City was about $4,000 in 1947 and about $5,200 in 1959 (both figures in terms of 1961 purchasing power). In other words, the modest but adequate level of living rose by 28 per cent in New York City in this twelve-year period—a growth rate of about 2 per cent per year.

[10] Robert Hunter, *Poverty* (New York: Macmillan, 1907), p. 52.

The essential fallacy of a fixed poverty line is that it fails to recognize the relative nature of "needs." The poor will not be satisfied with a given level of living year after year when the levels of those around them are going up at the rate of about 2.5 per cent per year. Old-timers may harken back to the "good old days" when people were happy without electricity, flush toilets, automobiles, and television sets; but they must also realize that, once it becomes possible for all to have these "luxuries," they will be demanded and will quickly assume the status of "needs." For these reasons, it is unrealistic in an expanding economy to think in terms of a fixed poverty line.

Recently, T. W. Schultz has attempted to use the elasticity concept borrowed from the theory of demand to explain the relationship between the rise in per capita income and the rise in the poverty line. He notes that the rise in the poverty line over time "represents an increase in the demand for welfare services for the poor, that this increase in demand as it is revealed by the social-political process is a function of the rise in per capita income which can be treated as income elasticity."[11] Schultz goes on to state that "the underlying behavior here is consistent with an income elasticity somewhat less than unity. During the period since the mid-thirties real income per family virtually doubled and the poverty line, measured in constant dollars, appears to have risen by 75 per cent."[12]

This formulation of the problem treats the poverty line in a way that is analogous to the treatment of other economic variables. For example, on the basis of empirical evidence we know that the relationship between aggregate income and saving behaves in a more or less predictable way over fairly long periods of time. Despite the persistent annual growth in per capita income during the past fifteen years the percentage of income saved has ranged between 6 and 8 per cent. This evidence suggests that as incomes have risen during the postwar period consumers have decided to devote a more or less constant proportion of that rise to savings. Analogously, we might find upon investigation, that there is a similar relationship between the level of income and the poverty line. If it is true, as Schultz alleges, that the percentage change in the poverty line is not as great as the percentage change in income, then we might expect on that account alone to find

---

[11] Theodore W. Schultz, "Investing in Poor People: An Economist's View," paper presented at the December 1964 meeting of the American Economic Association.

[12] This estimate is based on an unpublished study by Eugene Smolensky, "The Past and Present Poor," prepared by the U. S. Chamber of Commerce, quoted in Schultz, cited above.

a decrease in the incidence of poverty over time in a growing society. It was not too many years ago that Dorothy Brady stated before a congressional committee that "the attempts of investigators for more than half a century have apparently led to about the same answer to the question, 'what proportion of the population does not have a minimum standard of living?' "[13] We now seem to be coming up with a different answer to this question. Here certainly is a problem that deserves more attention than it has received.

Long-Run Changes in the Incidence of Poverty

Although the evidence is scanty, there seems to be general agreement that there has been an appreciable reduction in the incidence of poverty even when contemporary (rather than present) definitions of poverty are used. In reporting on changes during the post-war period, Oscar Ornati has used three different poverty lines: minimum subsistence defined as less than $2,500 per year in 1960; minimum adequacy which is less than $3,500; and minimum comfort, less than $5,500.[14] Using these concepts, with adjustments for changes in prices and standards over time, Ornati concludes that

> the proportion of the poor living below levels of minimum adequacy and minimum comfort has not changed very much. Indeed in 1947, by 1947 standards, 27.5 per cent of the people (that is of individuals living in households) lived below minimum adequacy levels and in 1960, by 1960 standards, 26 per cent were in this class. The proportion living below minimum comfort was 39 per cent in 1947, while in 1960 it was 40 per cent. The story is different when abject poverty is considered. Here, when the proportion living at or below minimum subsistence in 1947 is compared with the per cent barely subsisting in 1960, we find that the proportion decreased from 15 per cent to 11 per cent. [15]

These findings suggest that during the post-war period, at least, the rise in the "adequacy" line has kept pace with the rise in average income. Since there was no change in income distribution during this

---

[13] Statement of Dorothy Brady at *Hearings Before the Subcommittee on Low-Income Families*, Joint Committee on the Economic Report, 81st Congress, Sess. I, p.475.

[14] Oscar Ornati, "Affluence and the Risk of Poverty," *Social Research*, XXXI (Autumn, 1964), 334.

[15] *Ibid.* Details underlying these estimates are not given in the report cited. The report notes, however, that details will appear in a forthcoming publication of The Twentieth Century Fund by Oscar Ornati, *Poverty in the Affluent Society*.

period, the proportion of families living below the level of adequacy remained fairly constant. It appears, however, that the "poverty" line did not rise as rapidly as average income. Consequently, there was a drop in the proportion of families with incomes below the poverty line.

In an unpublished manuscript, Ruth Mack has attempted to extend our knowledge in this area back to 1929.[16] She uses three different poverty lines: a "low" poverty line based on budgets prepared by the New York Department of Welfare since 1934; a "high" poverty line based on the "modest but adequate" Heller budgets since 1920; and an "average" poverty line based on a variety of budgets that represent low, medium, and high poverty lines. For each year, the various poverty lines were compared with the income distributions for families of two or more persons prepared by the Office of Business Economics.

Dr. Mack's figures suggest that the incidence of poverty in the United States has been sharply reduced regardless of the poverty level that is used (Table 7). The most marked reduction appears to have taken place for those groups nearest the bottom of the income distribution. Even during the prosperous 1920's, it appears that about one-fourth of the families had incomes below what we might call a "subsistence" budget. That proportion increased somewhat during the Depression, was sharply reduced by the outbreak of the Second World War, and has been dropping ever since. In 1960, only about one-tenth of the families had incomes below this "subsistence" budget. It is interesting that the sharpest reductions in "abject" poverty appear to have taken place between the depths of the Depression and the outbreak of World War II. This period also coincides with a great rise in per capita income and the institution of various income maintenance measures introduced by the Roosevelt Administration. Both factors contributed to the very significant reduction in abject poverty during this period.

The proportion of families with incomes below the high poverty line, which some have called "deprivation," has also been reduced, but not as sharply as the proportion living in "abject" poverty. It appears

---

[16] Dr. Mack has generously given me permission to use the data cited here. These figures should be used with caution since I have omitted some of the qualifying conditions and the more detailed descriptions of the adjustment procedures contained in the original manuscript.

that about one-half of the families were "in deprivation" prior to World War II as compared with about one-third of the families during the post-war period. In view of the stability of income distribution

Table 7. *Per Cent of Families with Incomes below Various Poverty Lines, Based on Contemporary Definitions of Poverty, 1929–1960*

Year	Poverty line (1960 dollars)[a]			Per cent of families with incomes below each poverty line		
	Low	Average	High	Low	Average	High
1929	$1,960[b]	$2,531	$2,938	26	40	50
1935–36	1,741	2,735	3,787	28	48	65[c]
1941	1,613	2,638	3,707	17	33	48
1950	2,213	3,334	4,352	13	27	36
1960	2,422	3,827	5,104	10	21	35

[a] These figures have been adjusted for comparability with respect to changes in average size of family. Average family size was 4.0 in 1929; 3.9 in 1935–36; 3.7 in 1941; 3.5 in 1950; and 3.3 in 1960. On the basis of these averages, the poverty levels for each year were multiplied by the factors shown below. The factors used to convert *current dollars* to 1960 prices are also shown below:

Year	Adjustment factors	
	Size of family	Price changes
1929	1.00	58.0
1935–36	1.00	46.4
1941	.96	49.7
1950	.93	81.2
1960	.91	100.0

[b] This estimate is based on the budget compiled by the Community Service Society whereas the "low" poverty line for later years is based on the New York Welfare Department budgets. For this reason, the apparent decrease in the "low" poverty line between 1929 and 1935–36 may be spurious.

[c] Dr. Mack notes that this figure is out of line. The Heller budget on which it is based was revised in 1935 and sharply increased.

Source: Based on unpublished data provided by Dr. Ruth Mack, Institute of Public Administration, New York, New York.

since the early 1940's, it appears that the rise in the deprivation line has more closely approximated the rise in average incomes than has been the case for the subsistence poverty line.

The reduction in the incidence of poverty appears to be far greater than that shown above if the 1960 poverty lines are used for the earlier years. Table 8 shows that during the Depression nearly one-half of the families had incomes below the "subsistence" budget. This proportion dropped to about one-third at the outbreak of the Second

Table 8. *Per Cent of Families with Incomes below Various Poverty Lines, Based on 1960 Definitions of Poverty, 1929–1960*

Year	Families with incomes below poverty lines (%)		
	Low	Average	High
1929	36	70	80
1935–36	47	70	83
1941	31	53	70
1950	26	34	55
1960	10	22	35

Source: Unpublished data provided by Dr. Ruth Mack, Institute of Public Administration, New York, New York.

World War; it dropped further to about one-fourth by the end of the war; and in 1960 only one-tenth of the families were in "abject" poverty. The reduction in poverty during the 1950's appears to be far greater if the 1960 poverty lines rather than contemporary poverty lines are used. This fact suggests that there was a relatively small rise in the "low" poverty line relative to the rise in income during this period.

Eugene Smolensky, using data and estimating procedures that are different from those used by Ruth Mack, provides a somewhat different picture of the reduction in the incidence of poverty since the Depression. Smolensky attempts to establish a relationship between the "real minimum-comfort per capita" budget and real GNP per capita for different points in time. The results are shown in Table 9. The budgets are defined simply as those "that have been prepared at various times for New York City workers." On the basis of this evidence, Smolensky concludes that "the minimum-comfort budgets per capita have generally been around one-half of real gross national product per capita."[17]

Smolensky then assumes that the minimum-comfort estimates shown in the above table for New York City "accurately reflect the relative rise in welfare levels demanded by some national consensus,

---

[17] Smolensky, *op. cit.*, p. 8.

Table 9. Selected New York City Budgets and Real Gross National
Product, 1903–1959 (1954 Dollars)

Year	(1) Real minimum-comfort per capita	(2) Real GNP per capita	Ratio (1):(2)
1903–05	$ 527	$ 924	.57
1914	358	1,026	.35
1918	587	1,109	.53
1935	776	1,166	.67
1947	919	1,865	.49
1951	1,006	2,102	.48
1954	1,057	2,125	.50
1959	1,022	2,421	.42

Source: Unpublished study by Eugene Smolensky, "The Past and Present
Poor," prepared by the U. S. Chamber of Commerce.*

except for the 1935–1936 budget, which will be arbitrarily scaled down
to 50 per cent of gross national product per capita in these years, on
the grounds that the other budgets surrounding it tend to point to
that ratio." He then suggests that if $3,000 in 1959 is used as the
contemporary definition of poverty, "a poverty measure for each of the
years 1935 and 1947 can be constructed on the assumption that the
ratio of the 1935 and 1947 poverty limits for the nation as a whole
should be the same as the ratio of these years to 1959, evidenced in
the New York City budgets."[18] The results are shown in Table 10.

Table 10. Per Cent of Families with Incomes below the Poverty Line,
1935, 1947, and 1959 (Estimates are in 1959 Dollars)[a]

Year	Poverty line	Per cent of families below poverty line
1935	$1,710	32
1947	2,697	27
1959	3,000	23

[a] The estimates are based on a variable poverty line centered around a $3,000
value for 1959.

Source: Unpublished study by Eugene Smolensky, "The Past and Present
Poor," prepared by the U. S. Chamber of Commerce.*

[18] Ibid., p. 33.

* Printed by permission of the Task Force on Economic Growth and Opportunity,
Chamber of Commerce of the United States, the first report of the Task Force,
The Concept of Poverty, © 1965.

These figures suggest that about one-third of the families were in poverty in 1935 and about one-fifth were in poverty in 1959 using a variable poverty line centered around a $3,000 value for 1959. The estimates prepared by Ruth Mack suggest a much sharper reduction in poverty during the past thirty years than those prepared by Smolensky.

The Two Nations*

Michael Harrington

The United States in the sixties contains an affluent society within its borders. Millions and tens of millions enjoy the highest standard of life the world has ever known. This blessing is mixed. It is built upon a peculiarly distorted economy, one that often proliferates pseudo-needs rather than satisfying human needs. For some, it has resulted in a sense or spiritual emptiness, of alienation. Yet a man would be a fool to prefer hunger to satiety, and the material gains at least open up the possibility of a rich and full existence.

At the same time, the United States contains an underdeveloped nation, a culture of poverty. Its inhabitants do not suffer the extreme privation of the peasants of Asia or the tribesmen of Africa, yet the mechanism of the misery is similar. They are beyond history, beyond progress, sunk in a paralyzing, maiming routine.

The new nations, however, have one advantage: poverty is so general and so extreme that it is the passion of the entire society to obliterate it. Every resource, every policy, is measured by its effect on the lowest and most impoverished. There is a gigantic mobilization of the spirit of the society: aspiration becomes a national purpose that penetrates to every village and motivates a historic transformation.

But this country seems to be caught in a paradox. Because its poverty is not so deadly, because so many are enjoying a decent standard of life, there are indifference and blindness to the plight of the poor. There are even those who deny that the culture of poverty exists. It is as if Disraeli's famous remark about the two nations of the rich and the poor had come true in a fantastic fashion. At precisely that moment in

* Reprinted with permission of The Macmillan Company from *The Other America* by Michael Harrington; © Michael Harrington, 1962.

history where for the first time a people have the material ability to end poverty, they lack the will to do so. They cannot see; they cannot act. The consciences of the well-off are the victims of affluence; the lives of the poor are the victims of a physical and spiritual misery.

The problem, then, is to a great extent one of vision. The nation of the well-off must be able to see through the wall of affluence and recognize the alien citizens on the other side. And there must be vision in the sense of purpose, of aspiration: if the word does not grate upon the ears of a gentile America, there must be a passion to end poverty, for nothing less than that will do.

In this summary chapter, I hope I can supply at least some of the material for such a vision. Let us try to understand the other America as a whole, to see its perspective for the future if it is left alone, to realize the responsibility and the potential for ending this nation in our midst.

But, when all is said and done, the decisive moment occurs after all the sociology and the description is in. There is really no such thing as "the material for a vision." After one reads the facts, either there are anger and shame, or there are not. And, as usual, the fate of the poor hangs upon the decision of the better-off. If this anger and shame are not forthcoming, someone can write a book about the other America a generation from now and it will be the same, or worse.

I

Perhaps the most important analytic point to have emerged in this description of the other America is the fact that poverty in America forms a culture, a way of life and feeling, that it makes a whole. It is crucial to generalize this idea, for it profoundly affects how one moves to destroy poverty.

The most obvious aspect of this interrelatedness is in the way in which the various subcultures of the other America feed into one another. This is clearest with the aged. There the poverty of the declining years is, for some millions of human beings, a function of the poverty of the earlier years. If there were adequate medical care for everyone in the United States, there would be less misery for old people. It is as simple as that. Or there is the relation between the poor farmers and the unskilled workers. When a man is driven off the land because of the impoverishment worked by technological progress, he leaves one part of the culture of poverty and joins another. If something were done about the low-income farmer, that would immediately tell in the statistics of urban unemployment and the economic underworld. The same is true of the Negroes. Any gain for America's minorities will immediately be translated into an advance for all the unskilled workers. One cannot raise the bottom of a society without benefiting everyone above.

Indeed, there is a curious advantage in the wholeness of poverty. Since the other America forms a distinct system within the United States, effective action at any one decisive point will have a "multiplier" effect; it will ramify through the entire culture of misery and ultimately through the entire society.

Then, poverty is a culture in the sense that the mechanism of impoverishment is fundamentally the same in every part of the system. The vicious circle is a basic pattern. It takes different forms for the unskilled workers, for the aged, for the Negroes, for the agricultural workers, but in each case the principle is the same. There are people in the affluent society who are poor because they are poor; and who stay poor because they are poor.

To realize this is to see that there are some tens of millions of Americans who are beyond the welfare state. Some of them are simply not covered by social legislation: they are omitted from Social Security and from minimum wage. Others are covered, but since they are so poor they do not know how to take advantage of the opportunities, or else their coverage is so inadequate as not to make a difference.

The welfare state was designed during that great burst of social creativity that took place in the 1930's. As previously noted its structure corresponds to the needs of those who played the most important role in building it: the middle third, the organized workers, the forces of urban liberalism, and so on. At the worst, there is "socialism for the rich and free enterprise for the poor," as when the huge corporation farms are the main beneficiaries of the farm program while the poor farmers get practically nothing; or when public funds are directed to aid in the construction of luxury housing while the slums are left to themselves (or become more dense as space is created for the well-off).

So there is the fundamental paradox of the welfare state: that it is not built for the desperate, but for those who are already capable of helping themselves. As long as the illusion persists that the poor are merrily freeloading on the public dole, so long will the other America continue unthreatened. The truth, it must be understood, is the exact opposite. The poor get less out of the welfare state than any group in America.

This is, of course, related to the most distinguishing mark of the other America: its common sense of hopelessness. For even when there are programs designed to help the other Americans, the poor are held back by their own pessimism.

On one level this fact has been described in this book as a matter of "aspiration." Like the Asian peasant, the impoverished American tends to see life as a fate, an endless cycle from which there is no deliverance. Lacking hope (and he is realistic to feel this way in many cases), that famous solution to all problems—let us educate the poor—becomes less and less meaningful. A person has to feel that education will do something for him if he is to gain from it. Placing a magnificent school with a fine faculty in the middle of a slum is, I suppose, better than having a run-down building staffed by incompetents. But it will not really make a difference so long as the environment of the tenement, the family, and the street counsels the children to leave as soon as they can to disregard schooling.

On another level, the emotions of the other America are even more profoundly disturbed. Here it is not lack of aspiration and of hope; it is a matter of personal chaos. The drunkenness, the unstable marriages, the violence of the other America are not simply facts about individuals. They are the description of an entire group in the society who react this way because of the conditions under which they live.

In short, being poor is not one aspect of a person's life in this country, it is his life. Taken as a whole, poverty is a culture. Taken on the family level, it has the same quality. These are people who lack education and skill, who have bad health, poor housing, low levels of aspiration and high levels of mental distress. They are, in the language of sociology, "multiproblem" families. Each disability is the more intense because it exists within a web of disabilities. And if one problem is solved, and the others are left constant, there is little gain.

One might translate these facts into the moralistic language so dear to those who would condemn the poor for their faults. The other Americans are those who live at a level of life beneath moral choice, who are so submerged in their poverty that one cannot begin to talk about free choice. The point is not to make them wards of the state. Rather, society must help them before they can help themselves.

II

There is another view about the culture of poverty in America: that by the end of the seventies it will have been halved.

It is important to deal in some detail with this theory. To begin with, it is not offered by reactionaries. The real die-hards in the United

States do not even know the poor exist. As soon as someone begins to talk on the subject, that stamps him as a humanitarian. And this is indeed the case with those who look to a relatively automatic improvement in the lot of the other America during the next twenty years or so.

The second reason why this view deserves careful consideration is that it rests, to a considerable extent, upon the projection of inevitable and automatic change. Its proponents are for social legislation and for speeding up and deepening this process. But their very arguments could be used to justify a comfortable, complacent inaction.

So, does poverty have a future in the United States?

One of the most reasonable and sincere statements of the theme that poverty is coming to an end in America is made by Robert Lampman in the Joint Committee Study Paper "The Low-Income Population and Economic Growth." Lampman estimates that around 20 per cent of the nation, some 32 million people, are poor. (My disagreements with his count are stated in the Appendix.) And he writes, "By 1977–87 we would expect about 10 per cent of the population to have low-income status as compared to about 20 per cent now."

The main point in Lampman's relatively optimistic argument is that poverty will decline naturally with a continuing rate of economic growth. As the sixties begin, however, this assumption is not a simple one. In the post-war period, growth increased until about the mid-fifties. Then a falling off occurred. In each of the post-war recessions, the recovery left a larger reservoir of "normal" prosperity unemployment. Also, long-term unemployment became more and more of a factor among the jobless. There were more people out of work, and they stayed out of work longer.

In the first period of the Kennedy Administration, various economists presented figures as to what kind of government action was necessary so as really to attack the problem of depressed areas and low-income occupations. There were differences, of course, but the significant fact is that the legislation finally proposed was usually only a percentage of the need as described by the Administration itself. There is no point now in becoming an economic prophet. Suffice it to say that serious and responsible economists feel that the response of the society has been inadequate.

This has led to a paradoxical situation, one that became quite obvious when economic recovery from the recession began in the spring of 1961. The business indicators were all pointing upward: production and productivity were on the increase. Yet the human indexes of recession showed a tenacity despite the industrial gain. Unemployment remained at high levels. An extreme form of the "class unemployment" described earlier seemed to be built into the economy.

At any rate, one can say that if this problem is not solved the other America will not only persist; it will grow. Thus, the first point of the optimistic thesis strikes me as somewhat ambiguous, for it too quickly assumes that the society will make the needed response.

But even if one makes the assumption that there will be steady economic growth, that will not necessarily lead to the automatic elimination of poverty in the United States. J. K. Galbraith, it will be remembered, has argued that the "new" poverty demonstrates a certain immunity to progress. In making his projection of the abolition of half the culture of poverty within the next generation, Lampman deals with this point, and it is important to follow his argument.

Lampman rejects the idea that insular (or depressed-areas) poverty will really drag the poor down in the long run. As an example of this point, he cites the fact that the number of rural farm families with incomes of under $2,000 fell during the 1947–1957 period from 3.3 million to 2.4 million because of a movement off the farm.

This point illustrates the problem of dealing with simple statistics. A movement from the farm to the city, that is, from rural poverty to urban poverty, will show an upward movement in money income. This is true, among other reasons, because the money income of the urban poor is higher than that of the country poor. But this same change does not necessarily mean that a human being has actually improved his status, that he has escaped from the culture of poverty. As was noted in the chapter on the agricultural poor, these people who are literally driven off the land are utterly unprepared for city life. They come to the metropolis in a time of rising skill requirements and relatively high levels of unemployment. They will often enter the economic underworld. Statistically, they can be recorded as a gain, because they have more money. Socially, they have simply transferred from one part of the culture of poverty to another.

At the same time, it should be noted that although there has been this tremendous exodus of the rural poor, the proportion of impoverished farms in America's agriculture has remained roughly the same.

Then Lampman deals with Galbraith's theory of "case poverty," of those who have certain disabilities that keep them down in the culture of poverty. Here it should be noted again that Galbraith himself is somewhat optimistic about case poverty. He tends to regard the bad health of the poor, physical as well as mental, as being facts about them that are individual and personal. If this book is right, particularly in the discussion of the twisted spirit within the culture of poverty, that is not the case. The personal ills of the poor are a social consequence, not a bit of biography about them. They will continue as long as the environment of poverty persists.

But Lampman's optimism goes beyond that of Galbraith. He believes that disabilities of case poverty ("mental deficiency, bad health, inability to adapt to the discipline of modern economic life, excessive procreation, alcohol, insufficient education") are "moderated over time." And he takes as his main case in point education. "For example, average educational attainment levels will rise in future years simply because younger people presently have better education than older people. Hence, as the current generation of old people pass from the scene, the per cent of persons with low educational attainment will fall."

This is true, yet it is misleading if it is not placed in the context of the changes in the society as a whole. It is much more possible today to be poor with a couple of years of high school than it was a generation ago. As I have pointed out earlier, the skill level of the economy has been changing, and educational deficiency, if anything, becomes an even greater burden as a result. In this case, saying that people will have more education is not saying that they will escape the culture of poverty. It could have a much more ironic meaning: that America will have the most literate poor the world has ever known.

Lampman himself concedes that the aged are "immune" to economic growth. If this is the case, and in the absence of ranging and comprehensive social programs, the intrease in the number and percentage of the poor within the next generation will actually increase the size of the other America. Lampman also concedes that families with female heads are immune to a general prosperity, and this is another point of resistance for the culture of poverty.

Finally, Lampman is much more optimistic about "non-white" progress than the discussion in this book would justify. I will not repeat the argument that has already been given. Let me simply state the point baldly: the present rate of economic progress among the minorities is agonizingly slow, and one cannot look for dramatic gains from this direction.

Thus, I would agree with Galbraith that poverty in the sixties has qualities that give it a hardiness in the face of affluence heretofore unknown. As documented and described in this book, there are many special factors keeping the unskilled workers, the minorities, the agricultural poor, and the aged in the culture of poverty. If there is to be a way out, it will come from human action, from political change, not from automatic processes.

But finally, let us suppose that Lampman is correct on every point. In that case a generation of economic growth coupled with some social legislation would find America in 1987 with "only" 10 per cent of the nation impoverished. If, on the other hand, a vast and comprehensive program attacking the culture of poverty could speed up this whole development, and perhaps even abolish poverty within a generation, what is the reason for holding back? This suffering is such an abomination in a society where it is needless that anything that can be done should be done.

In all this, I do not want to depict Robert Lampman as an enemy of the poor. In all seriousness, the very fact that he writes about the subject does him credit: he has social eyes, which is more than one can say for quite a few people in the society. And second, Lampman puts forward "A Program to Hasten the Reduction of Poverty" because of his genuine concern for the poor. My argument with him is not over motive or dedication. It is only that I believe that his theory makes the reduction of poverty too easy a thing, that he has not properly appreciated how deeply and strongly entrenched the other America is.

In any case, and from any point of view, the moral obligation is plain: there must be a crusade against this poverty in our midst.

III

If this research makes it clear that a basic attack upon poverty is necessary, it also suggests the kind of program the nation needs.

First and foremost, any attempt to abolish poverty in the United States must seek to destroy the pessimism and fatalism that flourish in the other America. In part, this can be done by offering real opportunities to these people, by changing the social reality that gives rise to their sense of hopelessness. But beyond that (these fears of the poor have a life of their own and are not simply rooted in analyses of employment chances), there should be a spirit, an elan, that communicates itself to the entire society.

If the nation comes into the other America grudgingly, with the mentality of an administrator, and says, "All right, we'll help you people," then there will be gains, but they will be kept to the minimum; a dollar spent will return a dollar. But if there is an attitude that society is gaining by eradicating poverty, if there is a positive attempt to bring these millions of the poor to the point where they can make their contribution to the United States, that will make a huge difference. The spirit of a campaign against poverty does not cost a single cent. It is a matter of vision, of sensitivity.

Let me give an example to make this point palpable. During the Montgomery bus boycott, there was only one aim in the Negro community of that city: to integrate the buses. There were no speeches on crime or juvenile delinquency. And yet it is reported that the crime rate among Negroes in Montgomery declined. Thousands of people had been given a sense of purpose, of their own worth and dignity. On their own, and without any special urging, they began to change their personal lives; they became a different people. If the same elan could invade the other America, there would be similar results.

Second, this book is based upon the proposition that poverty forms a culture, an interdependent system. In case after case, it has been documented that one cannot deal with the various components of poverty in isolation, changing this or that condition but leaving the basic structure intact. Consequently, a campaign against the misery of the poor should be comprehensive. It should think, not in terms of this or that aspect of poverty, but along the lines of establishing new communities, of substituting a human environment for the inhuman one that now exists.

Here, housing is probably the basic point of departure. If there were the funds and imagination for a campaign to end slums in the United States, most of the other steps needed to deal with poverty could be integrated with it. The vision should be the one described in the previous chapter: the political, economic, and social integration of the poor with the rest of the society. The second nation in our midst, the other America, must be brought into the Union.

In order to do this, there is a need for planning. It is literally incredible that this nation knows so much about poverty, that it has made so many inventories of misery, and that it has done so little. The material for a comprehensive program is already available. It exists in congressional reports and the statistics of government agencies. What is needed is that the society make use of its knowledge in a rational and systematic way. As this book is being written, there are proposals for a Department of Urban Affairs in the Cabinet (and it will probably be a reality by the time these words are published). Such an agency could be the co-ordinating center for a crusade against the other America. In any case, if there is not planning, any attempt to deal with the problem of poverty will fail, at least in part.

Then there are some relatively simple things that could be done, involving the expansion of existing institutions and programs. Every American should be brought under the coverage of Social Security, and the payments should be enough to support a dignified old age. The principle already exists. Now it must be extended to those who need help the most. The same is true with minimum wage. The spectacle of excluding the most desperate from coverage must come to an end. If it did, there would be a giant step toward the elimination of poverty itself.

In every subculture of the other America, sickness and disease are the most important agencies of continuing misery. The *New York Times* publishes a list of the "neediest cases" each Christmas. In 1960 the descriptions of personal tragedy that ran along with this appeal involved the majority of cases the want of those who had been struck down by illness. If there were adequate medical care, this charity would be unnecessary.

Today the debate on medical care centers on the aged. And indeed, these are the people who are in the most desperate straits. Yet it would be an error of the first magnitude to think that society's responsibility begins with those sixty-five years of age. As has been pointed out several times, the ills of the elderly are often the inheritance of the earlier years. A comprehensive medical program, guaranteeing decent care to every American, would actually reduce the cost of caring for the aged. That, of course, is only the hardheaded argument for such an approach. More importantly, such a program would make possible a human kind of existence for everyone in the society.

And finally, it must be remembered that none of these objectives can be accomplished if racial prejudice is to continue in the United States. Negroes and other minorities constitute only 25 per cent of the poor, yet their degradation is an important element in maintaining the entire culture of poverty. As long as there is a reservoir of cheap Negro labor, there is a means of keeping the poor whites down. In this sense, civil rights legislation is an absolutely essential component in any campaign to end poverty in the United States.

In short, the welfare provisions of American society that now help the upper two-thirds must be extended to the poor. This can be done if the other Americans are motivated to take advantage of the opportunities before them, if they are invited into the society. It can be done if there is a comprehensive program that attacks the culture of poverty at every one of its strong points.

But who will carry out this campaign?

There is only one institution in the society capable of acting to abolish poverty. That is the federal government. In saying this, I do not rejoice, for centralization can lead to an impersonal and bureaucratic program, one that will be lacking in the very human quality so essential in an approach to the poor. In saying this, I am only recording the facts of political and social life in the United States.

The cities are not now capable of dealing with poverty, and each day they become even less capable. As the middle class flees the central urban area, as various industries decentralize, the tax base of the American metropolis shrinks. At the same time, the social and economic problems with which the city must deal are on the rise. Thus, there is not a major city in the United States that is today capable of attacking poverty on its own. On the contrary, the high cost of poverty is dragging the cities down.

The state governments in this country have a political peculiarity that renders them incapable of dealing with the problem of poverty. They are, for the most part, dominated by conservative rural elements. In every state with a big industrial population, the gerrymander has given the forces of rural conservatism two or three votes per person. So it is that the state legislatures usually take more money out of the problem areas than they put back into them. So it is that state governments are notoriously weighted in the direction of caution, pinchpenny economics, and indifference to the plight of the urban millions.

The various private agencies of the society simply do not have the funds to deal with the other America. And even the "fringe benefits" negotiated by unions do not really get to the heart of the problem. In the first place, they extend to organized workers in a strong bargaining position, not to the poor. And second, they are inadequate even to the needs of those who are covered.

It is a noble sentiment to argue that private moral responsibility expressing itself through charitable contributions should be the main instrument of attacking poverty. The only problem is that such an approach does not work.

So, by process of elimination, there is no place to look except toward the federal government. And indeed, even if there were alternate choices, Washington would have to play an important role, if only because of the need for a comprehensive program and for national planning. But in any case there is no argument, for there is only one realistic possibility: only the federal government has the power to abolish poverty.

In saying this, it is not necessary to advocate complete central control of such a campaign. Far from it. Washington is essential in a double sense: as a source of the considerable funds needed to mount a campaign against the other America, and as a place for co-ordination, for planning, and the establishment of national standards. The actual implementation of a program to abolish poverty can be carried out through myriad institutions, and the closer they are to the specific local area, the better the results. There are, as has been pointed out already, housing administrators, welfare workers, and city planners with dedication and vision. They are working on the local level, and their main frustration is the lack of funds. They could be trusted actually to carry through on a national program. What they lack now is money and the support of the American people.

There is no point in attempting to blueprint or detail the mechanisms and institutions of a war on poverty in the United States. There is information enough for action. All that is lacking is political will.

Thus the difficult, hardheaded question about poverty that one must answer is this: Where is the political will coming from? The other America is systematically under-represented in the government of the United States. It cannot really speak for itself. The poor, even in politics, must always be the object of charity (with the major exception of the Negroes, who, in recent times, have made tremendous strides forward in organization).

As a result of this situation, there is no realistic hope for the abolition of poverty in the United States until there is a vast social movement, a new period of political creativity. In times of slow change or of stalemate, it is always the poor who are expendable in the halls of Congress. In 1961, for instance, the laundry workers were dropped out of the minimum wage as part of a deal with the conservatives. Precisely because they are so poor and cruelly exploited, no one had to fear their political wrath. They, and others from the culture of poverty, will achieve the protection of the welfare state when there is a movement in this land so dynamic and irresistible that it need not make concessions.

For that matter, it is much easier to catalogue the enemies of the poor than it is to recite their friends.

All the forces of conservatism in this society are ranged against the needs of the other America. The ideologues are opposed to helping the poor because this can be accomplished only through an expansion of the welfare state. The small businessmen have an immediate self-interest in maintaining the economic underworld. The powerful agencies of the corporate farms want a continuation of an agricultural program that aids the rich and does nothing for the poor.

And now the South is becoming increasingly against the poor. In the days of the New Deal, the southern Democrats tended to vote for various kinds of social legislation. One of the most outspoken champions of public housing, Burnet Maybank, was a senator from South Carolina. For one thing, there is a southern tradition of being against Wall Street and big business; it is part of the farmers' hostility to the railroads and the Babylons of the big city. For another, the New Deal legislation did not constitute a challenge to the system of racial segregation in the South. But in the post-war period, this situation began to change. As industrialization came to the South, there was a growing political opposition to laws like minimum wage, to unions, and to other aspects of social change. The leaders of this area saw their depressed condition as an advantage. They could lure business with the promise of cheap, unorganized labor. They were interested in exploiting their backwardness.

The result was the strengthening of the coalition of southern Democrats and conservative northern Republicans. The northern conservatives went along with opposition to civil rights legislation. The southerners threw their votes into the struggle against social advance. It was this powerful coalition that exacted such a price in the first period of the Kennedy Administration. Many of the proposals that would have benefited the poor were omitted from bills in the first place, and other concessions were made in the course of the legislative battle. Thus poverty in the United States is supported by forces with great political and economic power.

On the other side, the friends of the poor are to be found in the American labor movement and among the middle-class liberals. The unions in the post-war period lost much of the elan that had characterized them in the thirties. Yet on questions of social legislation they remained the most powerful mass force committed to change in general, and to bettering the lot of the poor in particular. On issues like housing, medical care, minimum wage, and social security, the labor movement provided the strongest voice stating the cause of the poor.

Yet labor and the liberals were caught in the irrationalities of the American party system, and this was an enormous disdavantage to the other America. The unionists and their liberal allies are united in the Democratic party with the southern conservatives. A Democratic victory was usually achieved by appealing to those who were concerned for social change. But at the same time it brought the forces of conservatism powerful positions on the standing committees of the Congress.

Indeed, part of the invisibility of poverty in American life is a result of this party structure. Since each major party contained differences within itself greater than the differences between it and the other party, politics in the fifties and early sixties tended to have an issueless character. And where issues were not discussed, the poor did not have a chance. They could benefit only if elections were designed to bring new information to the people, to wake up the nation, to challenge, and to call to action.

In all probability there will not be a real attack on the culture of poverty so long as this situation persists. For the other America cannot be abolished through concessions and compromises that are almost inevitably made at the expense of the poor. The spirit, the vision that are required if the nation is to penetrate the wall of pessimism and despair that surrounds the impoverished millions cannot be produced under such circumstances.

What is needed if poverty is to be abolished is a return of political debate, a restructuring of the party system so that there can be clear choices, a new mood of social idealism.

These, then, are the strangest poor in the history of mankind.

They exist within the most powerful and rich society the world has ever known. Their misery has continued while the majority of the nation talked of itself as being "affluent" and worried about neuroses in the suburbs. In this way tens of millions of human beings became invisible. They dropped out of sight and out of mind; they were without their own political voice.

Yet this need not be. The means are at hand to fulfill the age-old dream: poverty can now be abolished. How long shall we ignore this underdeveloped nation in our midst? How long shall we look the other way while our fellow human beings suffer? How long?

Epilogue

On Buying and Selling*

Kahlil Gibran

AND a merchant said, Speak to us of Buying and Selling.

And he answered and said:

To you the earth yields her fruit, and you shall not want if you but know how to fill your hands.

It is in exchanging the gifts of the earth that you shall find abundance and be satisfied.

Yet unless the exchange be in love and kindly justice, it will but lead some to greed and others to hunger.

When in the market place you toilers of the sea and fields and vineyards meet the weavers and the potters and the gatherers of spices,—

Invoke then the master spirit of the earth, to come into your midst and sanctify the scales and the reckoning that weighs value against value.

And suffer not the barren-handed to take part in your transactions, who would sell their words for your labour.

---

* Reprinted from *The Prophet* by Kahlil Gibran with permission of the publisher, Alfred A. Knopf, Inc. Copyright, 1923 by Kahlil Gibran; renewal copyright 1951 by Administrators C.T.A. of Kahlil Gibran Estate, and Mary G. Gibran.

To such men you should say,
"Come with us to the field, or go with
our brothers to the sea and cast your net;
For the land and the sea shall be bountiful
to you even as to us."

And if there come the singers and the
dancers and the flute players,—buy of their
gifts also.
For they too are gatherers of fruit and
frankincense, and that which they bring,
though fashioned of dreams, is raiment
and food for your soul.

And before you leave the market place,
see that no one has gone his way with
empty hands.
For the master spirit of the earth shall
not sleep peacefully upon the wind till the
needs of the least of you are satisfied.